'Many people have a sense of unease about the direction in which AI is taking us. This is more than a worry about losing jobs or online content, although these are symptoms. This is a sense that something more fundamental is wrong—that the way programmers and designers understand 'intelligence' is itself awry.

With her extraordinary ability to bridge the arts and sciences, Eve Poole not only diagnoses what is wrong, but offers an entirely novel suggestion about how to put it right. Rather than throwing up her hands in horror, Poole offers a way out of the nightmare: stop stripping out all that makes us most human—like emotions and mistakes—and put our 'junk code' into the programming. If it has been good enough for human survival, it is good enough for AI.

Robot Souls is a brilliant book that wears its breadth of learning lightly and makes a complex subject seem simple. It is funny, readable, and important. It upends the fundamental presuppositions of AI and puts the enterprise on a new, more human, foundation.'

Linda Woodhead, *F.D.Maurice Professor*
King's College London, UK

'In *Robot Souls*, Eve Poole advances what is a provocative—even heretical—idea: our AIs and robots not only can have souls; we need them to have souls. In developing this groundbreaking proposal, Poole not only provides a much-needed critical examination of human exceptionalism but uses this opportunity to develop an innovative conceptualisation of soul as the messy but necessary "junk code" of consciousness. More than a report concerning the current and future state-of-the-art, this remarkable and thoroughly engaging book is a soul-searching meditation on the nature of the soul, the significance it has had for our own self-image as human beings, and the fact that we now are and must learn to be responsible for the souls of those artefacts that have been created in our image.'

David J. Gunkel, *Northern Illinois University, USA*

'What does it mean that humans are endowed with souls? Could souls be the markers of our distinctiveness from intelligent machines, or might robots also acquire them? These questions are critical in the context of the ongoing Artificial Intelligence revolution, and Eve Poole's *Robot Souls* engages them directly and skillfully at the interface between science and religion. Her 'junk code' proposal represents a bold and exciting hypothesis, making us rethink what we deem most important about being human.'

Marius Dorobantu, *The Vrije Universiteit Amsterdam, the Netherlands*

Robot Souls

Two of the biggest design problems in Artificial Intelligence are how to build robots that behave in line with human values and how to stop them ever going rogue. One under-explored solution to these alignment and control problems might be to examine how these are already addressed in the design of humans.

Looking closely at the human blueprint, it contains a suite of capacities that are so clumsy they have generally been kept away from AI. It was assumed that robots with features like emotions and intuition, that made mistakes and looked for meaning and purpose, would not work as well as robots without this kind of code. But on considering why all these irrational properties are there, it seems that they emerge from the source code of soul. Because it is actually this 'junk' code that makes us human and promotes the kind of reciprocal altruism that keeps humanity alive and thriving.

Robot Souls looks at developments in AI and reviews the emergence of ideas of consciousness and the soul. It places our 'junk code' in this context and argues that it is time to foreground that code, and to use it to look again at how we are programming AI.

Eve Poole has a BA from Durham, an MBA from Edinburgh, and a PhD from Cambridge. She has an OBE for services to education and gender equality and is a Life Fellow of the RSA. Following a career at Deloitte and Ashridge Business School, she was Chairman of Gordonstoun (2015–2021), Third Church Estates Commissioner for England (2018–2021), and Interim Chief Executive of the Royal Society of Edinburgh (2022). Her previous books include *Capitalism's Toxic Assumptions*, *Buying God*, and *Leadersmithing*, which was highly commended in the 2018 Business Book Awards.

Robot Souls
Programming in Humanity

Eve Poole

CRC Press
Taylor & Francis Group
Boca Raton London New York

CRC Press is an imprint of the
Taylor & Francis Group, **an informa** business

Designed cover image: © Shutterstock

First edition published 2024
by CRC Press
6000 Broken Sound Parkway NW, Suite 300, Boca Raton, FL 33487-2742

and by CRC Press
4 Park Square, Milton Park, Abingdon, Oxon, OX14 4RN

CRC Press is an imprint of Taylor & Francis Group, LLC

© 2024 Eve Poole

ISBN: 978-1-032-43285-4 (hbk)
ISBN: 978-1-032-42662-4 (pbk)
ISBN: 978-1-003-36661-4 (ebk)

DOI: 10.1201/9781003366614

Typeset in Minion
by codeMantra

For Professor Canon Ann Loades CBE
1938–2022

Contents

Preface, xi

Acknowledgements, xiii

CHAPTER 1 ▪ What Is AI?   1

   IS AI CONSCIOUS?   1

   ROBOTS   2

   INVENTING AI   2

   DEEP LEARNING   5

   REINFORCEMENT LEARNING   7

   BAYESIAN AI   9

   THE TURING TEST   10

   NOTES   11

CHAPTER 2 ▪ How Should We Relate to AI?   15

   HOW SHOULD WE TREAT AI?   15

   REGULATION   17

   LEGAL STATUS   20

   AUDIT   22

   ASIMOV 2.0   23

   NOTES   25

CHAPTER 3 ▪ Will AI Replace Us?   29

   OUR OBSOLESCENCE PROBLEM   29

   THE 12 DOOMS   30

DISTINCTIVENESS   32

MATERIALISM   33

FREE WILL AND THE RULE OF LAW   35

NOTES   36

CHAPTER 4 ■ What Is Consciousness?   39

MIND   39

CONSCIOUSNESS   42

QUALIA   44

NOTES   48

CHAPTER 5 ■ How Do We Know?   51

HOW WE KNOW THINGS   51

THINKING STYLES   54

TYPES OF INTELLIGENCE   57

NOTES   59

CHAPTER 6 ■ The Soul   63

HISTORY OF THE SOUL   64

MAPPING SOUL TO CONSCIOUSNESS   69

NOTES   71

CHAPTER 7 ■ Junk Code   73

JUNK CODE?   73

Emotions   74

Mistakes   77

Storytelling   79

Sixth Sense   82

Uncertainty   86

Free Will   88

Meaning   91

COMMUNITY   93

NOTES   94

CHAPTER 8 ■ Cultivating Soul   99

　　CULTIVATING JUNK CODE   99

　　　　Emotions   100

　　　　Mistakes   101

　　　　Storytelling   104

　　　　Sixth Sense   104

　　　　Uncertainty   105

　　　　Free Will   106

　　　　Meaning   108

　　NOTES   109

CHAPTER 9 ■ Programming in Humanity   111

　　WHY BOTHER?   111

　　PARENTING   113

　　GENDER   114

　　CODING SOUL?   115

　　　　Emotions   116

　　　　Mistakes   118

　　　　Storytelling   121

　　　　Sixth Sense   121

　　　　Uncertainty   122

　　　　Free Will   123

　　　　Meaning   124

　　ROBOT MANIFESTO   124

　　NOTES   125

CHAPTER 10 ■ Eucatastrophe   129

　　CHANGING OUR MINDS   129

　　HAPPILY EVER AFTER?   131

　　NOTES   134

APPENDIX, 135

GLOSSARY, 137

REFERENCES, 149

INDEX, 157

Preface

HUMANITY IS AT A crossroads. We have advanced far enough in our development of Artificial Intelligence to understand that we are in danger of losing control of it. We have already designed robots that can learn from scratch and be resourceful about finding any data they lack. We have also designed them to re-program themselves if they decide it would improve their ability to meet their objectives. This means that we are increasingly designing ourselves out of their lives.

At the moment, our freedoms are protected by a set of assumptions about the dignity of the human person that are actually rather hard to substantiate. Because we have not often had to define our humanity, we are not precise at doing so. And in a world where the regulation and control of Artificial Intelligence is of increasing concern, there is an urgent need to be able to be more precise.

One cypher that has been used in history to define humanity is to engage the concept of the soul. Today this is more familiar as the discussion of consciousness. But if consciousness is a pre-requisite for human rights, what happens if Artificial Intelligence becomes conscious?

This book reviews progress in Artificial Intelligence and examines the traditional debate on consciousness and the soul. It looks at how we might understand soul as the basis for human design, and discovers in it an array of code that is in danger of being overlooked. In particular, it argues that we have deliberately kept this 'junk code' away from Artificial Intelligence because we did not appreciate its value. The book concludes that we should instead identify, nurture, and promote this code as the defining feature of our humanity. Furthermore, we should seek to code it into Artificial Intelligence, not only because of its usefulness in design, but also because it is the right thing for us to do, to behave well towards the creatures we have made.

Acknowledgements

M Y THANKS TO: BARBARA Banda, Arkapravo Bhaumik, Jennifer Bihldorff, Malcolm Brown, Matt Clifford, Paul Davies, Rosie Dawson, Marius Dorobantu, Azariah France-Williams, Robert Geraci, Adam Gordon, Gordon Graham, Daina Habdankaite, James Harris, Philip Krinks, Hod Lipson, Lucy McClune, Jolyon Mitchell, Kim Morton, Tim Nash, Nathan Percival, Charles Rubin, Josh Smith, Robert Song, Stefan Stern, Linda Woodhead, James Woodward; to the Host community, the Norwich clergy, and Mr Eck's Lockdown Philosophy class; and to the University of Oxford's Committee for the Nomination of Select Preachers who first gave me the opportunity to preach on Robot Souls at the University Church in May 2019. I hereby certify that this book was written wholly by me and not by ChatGPT or any other AI.

CHAPTER 1

What Is AI?

It may be that today's large neural networks are slightly conscious.

Ilya Sutskever, Chief Scientist Open AI, 9 February 2022

IS AI CONSCIOUS?

In a lab at Columbia University back in 2017, Hod Lipson was working on a robot. It was a simple little thing, just four small mechanical legs, which had been tasked with moving to the other side of the room. It had been programmed using Deep Learning, which uses artificial neural networks and Reinforcement Learning so that robots can teach themselves. Lipson wanted to know if these legs could work out how to walk on their own. Lo and behold, after a few days, the robot had taken its first steps and achieved the goal. So Lipson removed one of the legs, to see if it could re-learn to walk with just three. It worked. Flushed with success, the team got the clever robot ready for a formal demonstration. They started tracking how it was using its neural network to learn, and discovered something unexpected. The robot had taught itself how to read their faces. It had realised that observer feedback was relevant data, and had decided to harvest it. Indeed, it had repurposed a neuron just for that task.[1] As humans we can see why this was a smart choice, because we have all stood around cheering on a toddler, and our feedback helps them learn how to walk too. Before this happened, we had thought that robots would not be able to develop what looks a lot like spontaneous self-awareness; or at least not for years to come, until we finally developed Artificial General Intelligence and a

DOI: 10.1201/9781003366614-1

1

super-intelligent 'brain' of such staggering complexity that consciousness would naturally emerge. But Lipson's robot is quite basic. Were we wrong?

Yes, and no. I think we were wrong to think that this kind of self-awareness is just a property of the living. Logically it must kick in whenever in its evolution an entity needs it to, in order to promote learning and progress. But self-awareness is still different from consciousness, and consciousness in turn is distinct from soul. And because these distinctions are very important, it is worth exploring how they relate. But first, how far has Artificial Intelligence (AI) already got in replacing us with robots?

ROBOTS

AI and robotics are often interchangeable in the public imagination, because AI is often depicted as embodied in robots or androids. We've been tinkering with robots for centuries. According to Hesiod, even the ancient Greek God Hephaestus created automata, notably a giant bronze man called Talos, who protected the island of Crete by marching around the island three times a day, hurling boulders at enemy ships. Clockwork powered a trend for automata in the European courts of the late Renaissance, and the Victorian enthusiasm for mechanical marvels is now forever celebrated in the SF sub-genre steampunk. Myths about bringing things to life recur throughout history: Pygmalion's statue in Ovid's Metamorphoses, the puppet Pinocchio becoming a real boy thanks to the Blue Fairy, and even Frankenstein's monster. Gods, fairies, or scientists are usually involved in these animations or resurrections, and they do not always end well.[2]

Robotics in general has become a vital part of many manufacturing processes, and we are used to seeing pictures of machines making other machines. We are also used to seeing robotics increasingly deployed in surgery. Many of these are sophisticated but essentially mechanical extensions of the physical capacities of the operator, although they are increasingly being programmed to think as well. Many robots are now programmed to work autonomously, and some are also deliberately designed to look humanoid as well as to use cognitive algorithms. We are increasingly seeing these kinds of robots being used as companions for the elderly in countries like Japan. An uncomfortable milestone was reached in October 2017, when the Saudi Arabian state awarded citizenship to the humanoid social robot Sophia.[3]

INVENTING AI

How did we get here? Imagine you are tasked with inventing AI. To start with, you need to accomplish three foundational intellectual leaps.[4] The first pivotal step is to conceive of thought as a process, and not simply as a spontaneous phenomenon of some mysterious and nebulous kind. We owe this innovation to Thomas Hobbes. In his 1651 *Leviathan*, he starts his famous work of political economy off with his account of human nature. Based on his view of the body as a machine, he introduces the concept of 'trains of thought,' and the idea of rationality as 'computation.' Arguing that our thoughts are just like the 'reckoning' of additions and subtractions, he establishes the vital theoretical foundation for AI that human thought is a process.[5]

Next, you need to imagine that the thoughts of every person could be expressed in some kind of universal way, in order to surmount the international language barrier. Gottfried Leibniz made this leap for us, in identifying the universal language as the language of mathematics. In 1705, inspired by the hexagrams in the Chinese text the *I Ching*, he invented the binary system as his *characteristica universalis*, which became the source of modern Binary Code.[6]

Now we have two of our vital foundations: thoughts are processes, that can be mathematically expressed. Finally, in order for AI to be possible, you need to make the intellectual leap that if numbers are the universal language, then any computational machine that processes numbers can process anything else that can be expressed in numbers. In the 19th century, Ada Lovelace provides this crucial piece of the puzzle. In 1833, her friend Charles Babbage had invented an Analytical Engine, hailed as the first programmable computer, and Lovelace was charged with translating a description of it from French. Babbage's machine used the kind of punch cards deployed in cloth factories to program Jacquard looms, and this made her realise that if programs could be used for both mathematics and weaving, perhaps anything susceptible to being rendered in logic – like music – could also be processed by a machine. Her 'Notes' describing the Engine were published in *Taylor's Scientific Memoirs* in 1843 and, as Doron Swade puts it, for the first time expressed the 'fundamental transition from a machine which is a number cruncher to a machine for manipulating symbols according to rules that is the fundamental transition from calculation to computation.'[7]

So now we have thoughts as processes, that can be expressed universally as numbers, that can be processed by a machine. With these foundation stones in place, the fun can begin. How on earth do we get from Jacquard looms and Babbage machines to Deep Blue and AlphaGo?

This requires a two-pronged evolution in both the hardware and the software involved. First, in hardware it requires the transition from the massive mechanical machines that decrypted the Enigma codes to the tiny ubiquitous smartphone. This move from mechanics to electronics marries a gradual reduction in size with an exponential increase in power. This was pioneered in the 1940s and 1950s through the use of silicon in both transistors (the equivalent of the 'off and on' mechanical switches that speak binary) and microchips (the wafer holding the miniaturised transistors). Silicon is a semiconductor that permits the particular manipulation of an electrical current (hence 'electronics') to boost both the number of transactions possible and the power needed to execute them. The rapid advances in computing that the miniaturisation of this technology has generated gave rise to 'Moore's Law:' in 1965, Gordon Moore, the co-founder of the chip manufacturer Intel, predicted that the number of transistors on a microchip would double every two years, while the cost of computers would halve.

The hardware was nearly ready. But now to the software: how did programming develop from punch cards to the kinds of algorithms that can crash stock markets? This requires advances in both the kind of program language used, and in the mathematical complexity of it. The first programs were written in 'machine code' which uses numbers to express basic instructions, cast in the kind of binary language that Leibniz would recognise. Frustrated by the highly detailed and arduous nature of this hand-coding process, in 1957 John Backus and his team at IBM developed a symbolic programming language called FORTRAN, by combining a form of English shorthand with algebraic equations. Other high-level general purpose programming languages followed, each trying to make the task of programming more efficient and accessible. Sophisticated decision logics were also developed, to add more intelligence into the process. From the highly mechanical programs that required hands-on human intervention, programs evolved to become 'expert systems' which could interrogate data and make independent decisions. Increasingly they also used natural language programming, such that nowadays young children can build their own cartoons in an intuitive program called Scratch.[8]

Meanwhile, the mathematics was also progressing at pace. In 1854, George Boole invented what is now a foundational logic in programming, because his algebra was used to solve the problem of optimising the use of switches. Claude Shannon at MIT (1937) and Victor Shestakov at Moscow State University (1941) both identified Boolean algebra as the key to deploying electrical switches to process logic, the basic concept that underlies the digital circuit design in all modern computing. On top of this foundational logic sits a welter of mathematical constructs to govern the now complex array of different problems being solved by AI. These instructions are generally nested in specific algorithms, which are programs that instruct a computer or other AI to follow a specified process or set of rules for calculations or other problem-solving tasks, expressed in one of the programming languages referred to earlier. As we shall see, it is these algorithms in particular which drive AI and have fuelled its progress. In this context, the UN's World Commission on the Ethics of Scientific Knowledge and Technology has drawn a distinction between 'deterministic robots' and 'cognitive robots.' While both are programmed with algorithms, the former use prescribed deterministic algorithms to control predictive behaviour; while cognitive robots are programmed with 'stochastic algorithms' which include learning functionality that makes their behaviour ultimately unpredictable.[9] In recent years, the work of the 18th-century statistician Thomas Bayes has also reached prominence in AI, because his 1763 thinking on probability has become key to Machine Learning, to which we shall return.

DEEP LEARNING

The advent of Machine Learning algorithms in the 1960s gave AI the ability to automatically self-improve through experience. Machine Learning is the general term for the development of algorithms in AI that drive its autonomous development, using training data to enable the AI to make future predictions or decisions without being explicitly programmed to do so. Deep Learning has now taken this to a level of complexity that has produced a step-change in the progress of AI. Deep Learning is a term that has been popularised by Geoffrey Hinton and others since 2006, although more basic multi-linear Machine Learning networks have formally existed since the 1960s.[10] Deep Learning was inspired by the discovery in the 1960s of the interplay between the simple and the complex cells in the visual cortex. These fire differentially in response to visual sensory inputs, and work as a team to identify the object in view. This insight informed the design of the artificial neural network architectures used in modern Deep Learning, which establish layers of problem-solving between artificial 'neurons,' and a division of labour by layer, with multiple relationships and iterations between them, to optimise data processing.[11] This architecture allows AI to move on from step-by-step problem-solving by simulating the fast and intuitive judgements that humans use to recognise patterns and anomalies.[12]

The early Deep Learning programs rejoiced in some dramatic names. In 1979, Kunihiko Fukushima built the Neocognitron which used a hierarchical, multi-layered artificial neural network to recognise handwritten Japanese characters and other patterns;[13] and in 1992 Weng et al. built the Cresceptron, which learned image-recognition from watching video images.[14] They failed to achieve the processing efficiency of the biological brain, so progress was comparatively slow until innovation in the gaming industry turbo-charged the next phase. A bit like the snowboarding industry transforming ski technology, the advent of cheap, multiprocessor graphics cards for gaming – Graphics Processing Units (GPUs) – fuelled improvements in Deep Learning. Their suitability for creating complex virtual realities also made GPUs perfect for artificial neural network training, where they can make learning 50 times faster.[15]

A further acceleration was achieved through an innovation called Supervised Long Short-Term Memory (LSTM) Recurrent Neural Networks. These are good at remembering and discovering the importance of events that happened thousands of processing steps ago, and it was one of these so-called LSTMs that at the 10th International Conference on Document Analysis and Recognition in 2009, won three connected cursive handwriting character recognition tests in three different languages (French, Arab, Farsi), without any previous linguistic knowledge, by performing simultaneous segmentation and recognition.[16]

Also in 2009, a Recurrent Neural Network taught itself to drive a simulated car using training videos, learning both control and visual processing from scratch.[17] In 2011, a further milestone was reached, in the area of traffic sign recognition, which is important for the programming of autonomous cars. Using a snappily named Max-Pooling Convolutional Neural Network powered by gaming processors, the program achieved a 0.56% error rate which was twice better than that achieved by human test subjects.[18] A year later saw advances in medical image processing, when a Deep Learning program won a contest on visual object detection at the flagship conference of the International Association of Pattern Recognition, being able to detect mitosis in breast cancer histological images, which should vastly improve the medical profession's ability to speed up diagnosis.[19] And speech recognition has also dramatically improved over recent years, thanks to the use of neural networks for speaker recognition, as pioneered by the Stanford Research Institute (SRI). The SRI's deep neural network was deployed for the first time commercially in the year 2000 in the company Nuance Communications' Verifier system (now being acquired by Microsoft). In 2015, Google announced that it had also massively improved performance by incorporating the neural network approach of Deep Learning into Google Voice Search.[20]

After the computer program Deep Blue became the chess word champion in 1996/7[21] – and another IBM computer called Watson won $1m on the US quiz show Jeopardy! in 2011[22] – Deep Learning has increasingly been applied to games, most famously to tackle the seemingly intractable intellectual challenge of winning the game Go.[23] Originating in China over 3,000 years ago, Go involves two players using black or white stones, taking turns to place their stones on a board. The aim is to surround and capture their opponent's stones, or to create territory. Once the game is over, the stones and the empty points are counted, and the person with the highest number wins. While the rules are simple, in mathematical terms it is extremely complex. As the DeepMind website puts it: 'there are an astonishing 10 to the power of 170 possible board configurations – more than the number of atoms in the known universe. This makes the game of Go a googol (1×10^{100}) times more complex than chess.'[24] The neural network approach of Deep Learning is particularly suitable for handling a problem of such computational scale. Using a combination of a neural network devoted to 'policy' about the next move balanced by a 'value' neural network charged with predicting who will win the overall game, AlphaGo was trained by playing both with human amateurs and with itself, using Reinforcement Learning. AlphaGo has famously defeated a series of Go world champions globally and is still being updated, making South Korean Lee Se-dol, a 9-dan Go master, the only human to have ever beaten AlphaGo.[25]

In 2020, Deep Mind's sister program AlphaFold 2 showed that it could determine the 3D shapes of proteins from their amino-acid sequence, thus solving the 'protein folding problem' that has stumped biologists for over 50 years. This was not only a milestone for AI, but for science. Determining their structure allows scientists to understand the physical interactions within the proteins, as well as their evolutionary history. This breakthrough has vastly accelerated efforts to understand how signals are transmitted across cell membranes, and will help scientists to identify malfunctioning proteins and how they interact, which will improve drug discovery. In July 2021, Deep Mind released AlphaFold on the internet so that it could be used by everybody.

REINFORCEMENT LEARNING

The field of Deep Learning has been generally improved by the widespread integration of Reinforcement Learning, such as that used in Go and the car driving example, whereby a program learns autonomously in an interactive environment, using trial-and-error feedback from its own actions and experiences. Reinforcement Learning uses 'rewards' and 'punishment' as signals for positive and negative behaviour. When AI is trained on competitive games, this is easily achieved through the scoring of points and the use of win/lose scenarios. Otherwise, the programmer needs to identify a scheme of reward for the task that does not accidentally incentivise truant behaviour. This is expressed as a number, and the program is told to maximise this number, with 'negative' rewards being used to correct mistakes. This use of reward signals to formalise programming goals is the distinctive feature of Reinforcement Learning; but as with children it is fraught with challenge: rewarding AI for chess pieces won rather than for winning the whole game is like children learning to skip through quick-reads rather than long books, if they are rewarded by quantity and not quality.[26]

One cautionary tale about getting the reinforcement structure wrong in unsupervised autonomous AI is the story of the launch of Microsoft's Tay twitter-bot on March 23, 2016. It took only 16 hours before the account had to be shut down. Having started with benign tweets, it quickly learned that it could get more attention by tweeting offensive and controversial content, and 95,000 tweets later it was terminated. Microsoft blamed this PR disaster on 'trolls,' but of course if you program AI to seek popularity that is exactly what it will do. This is because Deep Learning relies on 'fast, greedy learning algorithms'[27] that prioritise quantity over quality. If in analysing millions of tweets the AI learned that most of them were extreme and that this promoted popularity within its target segment, why would it pay attention to the minority of less popular but more wholesome accounts?[28]

Good Reinforcement Learning will pay attention to both the what *and* the how.[29] This also helps with the need for transparency in the programming of AI. Autonomous neural networks are not easy to track, but at least a clear reinforcement structure would permit audit. This means that bespoke reward structures may be optimal, although there are already general Reinforcement Learning designs available for universal problem-solving AI programs. One example is Jürgen Schmidhuber's Godel Machine, which rewrites any part of its own code as soon as it has found proof that a rewrite might be useful.[30] This is obviously worrying in the context of discussion about kill-switches and control, because of the need to be able to turn rogue AI off.[31]

BAYESIAN AI

In 2016, when *Wired* editor Scott Dadich asked Barack Obama if he was worried about AI going rogue, the then US President said, 'you just have to have somebody close to the power cord.'[32] This is the idea behind 'kill-switches.' One of the more troubling risks of autonomous AI is what happens when it gets so certain that it does the catastrophically wrong thing. As Obama said, the only recourse we then have is human intervention, but the whole point of AI is that it might be too intelligent for us to be able to stop it. Given that we are fallible and may not have programmed AI for every single nuance and eventuality, how do we mitigate this risk? Luckily, the AI community has been giving this a lot of thought, and has come up with a clever way to address it, by applying Bayesian logic to Deep Learning.

Bayesian AI operates by playing off the neurons in an artificial neural net against each other, so that they essentially average out. Suppose you have programmed a computer to categorise images by cat or dog, but some images are blurry, or erroneously included from another data set. What you do not want is the computer to force a category on a faulty image that is incorrect. But if it has no categories other than cat or dog to use, either you need to include an 'open category' or you need to add in a measure of doubt. Bayesian AI uses the wisdom of crowds to task all the neurons with categorising the image, so that the consensus image has a % probability attached to it, depending on the degree of agreement. In, say, medical imaging, variable agreement would trigger human intervention to ensure that wrong classifications are not assigned. Similarly, a low certainty score could be used to trigger a 'go slow' to buy more time.

In his book *The Alignment Problem*, Brian Christian also talks about a project inspired by the Japanese game sokoban. Sokoban is a puzzle about manoeuvring boxes in a warehouse, a bit like the old plastic sliding squares games from Christmas crackers. As in solitaire or the rubik's cube, if you proceed too directly, you often end up boxed into a corner. A more prudent path is to hedge your bets by taking a route that keeps your options open. In the same way, it would be useful if there was a way to head the AI off at the pass before a final decision becomes inevitable, and this insight has given rise to the invention of a new process to try to build in this kind of strategic flexibility.[33] All of these measures are designed to cater for doubt, something that is, by definition, programmed out of AI. Ironically, it then needs to be programmed straight back in to manage risk because, as all hillwalkers know, the map is never the territory.

THE TURING TEST

How will we know when AI has achieved human-level intelligence? The landmark test for this was devised by Alan Turing in a 1950 paper in which he asked the question, can machines think?[34] Accordingly, he introduced the idea of an 'imitation game' and suggested that a computer could be deemed to be 'thinking' if it were able to fool a person into thinking it was a fellow human. Over the years, there have been several attempts to replace the Turing Test with something more rigorous. The Chinese Room, which we will meet later, was one attempt to show that the Turing Test does not test *thinking* as much as apparently thoughtful outputs: a search engine may present you with data to rival the best archivist or librarian, but it has not *thought* about it. Nevertheless, the Turing Test still prevails in the public imagination, and the global Loebner Prize introduced as late as 1991 uses it to test the progress of AI. No machine has yet won silver or gold, but several have achieved bronze for the 'most human' conversation. The death of its sponsor has made it unclear whether after the last competition in 2019 there will be any opportunity to win gold in the future, so the field stands open for another way of benchmarking progress.[35] Meanwhile, the Turing Test seems daily to be passed by a succession of increasingly sophisticated chatbots. In 2022, Google sacked one of its employees for claiming that its chatbot LaMDA had 'become sentient' which certainly suggests he was at least fooled in precisely the way Turing intended.[36]

One modern test of which we are all aware is the 'CAPTCHA' that appears as part of an online authentication protocol, when you are asked to confirm that 'I am not a robot.' This test is devised to prevent hacking and fraud. CAPTCHAs are an intriguing puzzle because they need to be capable of being automatically generated and checked by AI, but only solvable by a human. CAPTCHA is a contrived acronym for Completely Automated Public Turing test to tell Computers and Humans Apart and is a type of challenge/response test used online to determine whether or not the user is human. Because AI is improving all the time, the tests have to keep improving too. First-generation CAPTCHAs were wonky words, often with variegated backgrounds, but these became too hackable. Next, some enterprising person at Carnegie Mellon realised that this free human identification service could be put to good use, and reCAPTCHA was sold to Google to use to help decipher compromised sections of old books. Currently, third generation CAPTCHAs tend to involve photo identification (also helpful free data!) like clicking on all the photographs that contain a cat.[37] These tests end up being a bellwether for the race between humans and AI and the pace at which they are currently changing is a measure of how fast AI is catching up.

NOTES

1 From the 2018 documentary *Do You Trust this Computer?* at http://doyoutrustthiscomputer.org/ and cited in Glattfelder, James B (2019) *Information—Consciousness—Reality*, New York, NY: Springer, p550.

2 For an excellent brief history of robotics and AI see p12–14 of the COMEST report on Robotics Ethics at https://unesdoc.unesco.org/ark:/48223/pf0000253952.

3 See https://www.wired.co.uk/article/sophia-robot-citizen-womens-rights-detriot-become-human-hanson-robotics.

4 See Dreyfus, Hubert L (1992) *What Computers Still Can't Do*, Cambridge, MA: MIT Press, pp69ff.

5 Hobbes, Thomas (2017) *Leviathan*, London: Penguin, p20 and 30.

6 His 1705 article 'Explication de l'Arithmétique Binaire' was published in the journal of the French Academy of Sciences, see Antognazza, Maria Rosa (ed) (2021) *The Oxford Handbook of Leibniz*, Oxford: OUP, p244.

7 Fuegi, John & Francis, John (2003) 'Lovelace & Babbage and the creation of the 1843 'notes,"' *IEEE Annals of the History of Computing* 25, p16–26.

8 Dickins, Rosie (2015) *Computers and Coding*, London: Usborne.

9 See p4 of the COMEST report on Robotics Ethics at https://unesdoc.unesco.org/ark:/48223/pf0000253952.

10 See history in section 5.15 of Schmidhuber, Jürgen (2015) 'Deep learning in neural networks: An overview,' *Neural Networks* 61, p85–117.

11 For a wonderful story about the underlying discovery of the logic of neurons, see the Prologue in Christian, Brian (2020) *The Alignment Problem*, London: Atlantic books, p1–3.

12 Modern artificial neural networks can 'think' a lot faster than biological ones, because they are made from non-biological materials that facilitate the faster movement of protons; see the advent of nanoscale protonic programmable resistors in Onen, M, Emond, N, Wang, B, Zhang, D, Ross, Li, J, FM, Yildiz, B & Del Alamo JA (2022) 'Nanosecond protonic programmable resistors for analog deep learning.' *Science* 377:6605, p539–543.

13 Fukushima, K (1980) 'Neocognitron: a self-organizing neural network model for a mechanism of pattern recognition unaffected by shift in position,' *Biological Cybernetics* 36, p193–202.

14 Weng, J, Ahuja, N, and Huang, TS (1992) 'Cresceptron: a self-organizing neural network which grows adaptively,' *International Joint Conference on Neural Networks* 1, p576–581.

15 See section 4.5 of Schmidhuber, Jürgen (2015) 'Deep learning in neural networks: An overview,' *Neural Networks* 61, p85–117.

16 See section 5.17 of Schmidhuber, ibid.

17 Loiacono, D, Lanzi, PL, Togelius, J, Onieva, E, Pelta, DA, Butz, MV, Lonneker, TD, Cardamone, L, Perez, D, Saez, Y, Preuss, M & Quadflieg, J (2010) 'The 2009 simulated car racing championship,' *IEEE Transactions on Computational Intelligence and AI in Games* 2:2.

18 Sermanet, P and LeCun, Y (2011) 'Traffic sign recognition with multi-scale convolutional networks,' *Proceedings of the International Joint Conference on Neural Networks,* p2809–2813.

19 Roux, L, Racoceanu, D, Lomenie, N, Kulikova, M, Irshad, H, Klossa, J, Capron, F, Genestie, C, Naour, GL, & Gurcan, MN (2013) 'Mitosis detection in breast cancer histological images - an ICPR 2012 contest' *Journal of Pathology Informatics* 4:1, p8.

20 See https://ai.googleblog.com/2015/09/google-voice-search-faster-and-more.html.

21 Deep Blue was the name of the IBM computer that beat the world champion Garry Kasparov in a chess game in 1996. By beating him over a series of games the following year, Deep Blue became the first computer system to defeat a reigning world champion in a match under standard chess tournament time controls.

22 Watson also unfortunately learned how to swear: https://www.ibtimes.com/ibms-watson-gets-swear-filter-after-learning-urban-dictionary-1007734.

23 Gaming milestones continue to be made by AI, with further breakthroughs in Diplomacy and Stratego reported in 2022. See Cicero on Diplomacy in Bakhtin, A, Brown, N, Dinan, E, Lewis, M et al (2022) 'Human-level play in the game of Diplomacy by combining language models with strategic reasoning' *Science* 378:6624, p1067–1074 and DeepNash on Stratego in Perolat et al (2022) 'Mastering the game of Stratego with model-free multiagent reinforcement learning' *Science* 378:6623, p990–996; doi: 10.1126/science.add467.

24 See the AlphaGo case study at https://deepmind.com/research/case-studies/alphago-the-story-so-far.

25 He has since retired, believing that his lone victory in 2016 was simply due to a bug in its programming, see https://www.theverge.com/2019/11/27/20985260/ai-go-alphago-lee-se-dol-retired-deepmind-defeat.

26 See the story of Amodei's spinning boat in Christian, Brian (2020) *The Alignment Problem,* London: Atlantic books, p9f.

27 See Hinton, GE, Osindero, S, & Teh, Y-W (2006) 'A fast learning algorithm for deep belief nets' *Neural Computation* 18:7, 1527–1554.

28 See for example coverage at https://spectrum.ieee.org/in-2016-microsofts-racist-chatbot-revealed-the-dangers-of-online-conversation.

29 Sutton, RS, Barto, AG & Bach F (2018) *Reinforcement Learning: An Introduction,* 2nd Edition, Cambridge, MA: MIT Press, p53f.

30 Schmidhuber, J (2007) 'Gödel machines: fully self-referential optimal universal self-improvers,' *Cognitive Technologies* 8, p199–226.

31 Spoiler alert: the plot of Dan Brown's 2017 book *Origin* (London: Penguin) is a cautionary tale about incorrect RL – an assassinated author and a conspiracy theory would sell more books.

32 As quoted in Christian, Brian (2020) *The Alignment Problem*, London: Atlantic, p296. See the full 2016 interview here: https://www.wired.com/2016/10/president-obama-mit-joi-ito-interview/.

33 Christian, Brian (2020) *The Alignment Problem*, London: Atlantic, p293, on 'stepwise relative reachability.' See also p283–288 on Bayesian AI; and the work of the Queen Mary Bayesian Artificial Intelligence research lab at https://bayesian-ai.eecs.qmul.ac.uk/.

34 Turing, AM (1950) 'Computing machinery and intelligence,' *Mind* 59, p433–460.

35 See https://www.bbc.co.uk/news/technology-49578503.

36 As reported in the Washington Post on 22 July 2022: https://www.washingtonpost.com/technology/2022/07/22/google-ai-lamda-blake-lemoine-fired/.

37 See https://www.theverge.com/2019/2/1/18205610/google-captcha-ai-robot-human-difficult-artificial-intelligence.

CHAPTER 2

How Should We Relate to AI?

Our machines are disturbingly lively, and we ourselves frighteningly inert.

Donna Haraway

HOW SHOULD WE TREAT AI?

It has been customary in thinking about the ethics of AI in the past to focus on what we suppose AI might warrant or deserve in terms of status or treatment. A better question, however, is to ask what kind of humans we want to be, in relation to AI. Using the first logic, we might game all kinds of scenarios about robot ethics designed to ensure that humans prevail, but the second logic asks us to park our paranoia about control and instead work out who we want to be, and how we want to characterise our relationships with AI. This is certainly the argument put forth by the robot rights pioneer David Gunkel in suggesting a more relational approach to the debate, based on the thinking that rights arise not from an entity itself but from its social context.[1]

That said, Nick Bostrom, writing with Eliezer Yudkowsky, sets out two clear criteria for our treatment of AI, arguing that it should have full moral status if it has both Sentience (the capacity for phenomenal experience such as the capacity to feel pain and suffer) and Sapience (a set of capacities associated with higher intelligence, such as self-awareness and being a reason-responsive agent).[2] This is certainly the subtext of the advice to

DOI: 10.1201/9781003366614-2

UNESCO on robotics ethics, that if robot agency progresses much further (sapience), and AI learns how to feel emotions (sentience), there would need to be provision made for some new kind of moral personality and protection in law, in the same way that we have awarded protections to animals on the basis of their sentience alone.[3] In the case of moral culpability, this would require debate on what kind of consequences, sanctions or reparation would most appropriately apply to AI.

Bostrom goes on to argue that AI like any other entity would deserve full moral status because of two particular principles which naturally follow. If AI has the same functionality and the same conscious experience as us, then regardless of whether they share the same 'substrate of implementation' they should have the same moral status as us (his Principle of Substrate Non-Discrimination). And if we share the same functionality and the same conscious experience, and differ only in how we came into existence, then they merit the same moral status regardless (his Principle of Ontogeny Non-Discrimination). He argues that 'whether somebody is implemented on silicon or biological tissue, if it does not affect functionality or consciousness, is of no moral significance. Carbon-chauvinism is objectionable on the same grounds as racism.'[4]

Apart from any argument from the point of view of the rights of the robot, there is a strong argument from the point of view of our responsibility as its creator. The Philosopher Mary Midgley has always warned against confusion in language. We should not anthropomorphise machines because that is to commit the category mistake of confusing them with people.[5] We should also be alive to the tendency in humans for transference and projection. This gets progressively worse the more our AI develops 'social valency' because we make friends with our robots. Then, as Sergio Avila Negri argues, we start to think of robots as if they were people, and 'we envisage for the artefact a degree of agency and autonomy that is not simply exaggerated, it is actually a transference, in which we lose part of our own autonomy.'[6] That said, we created these entities, and we programmed them for our use. If at some stage they become sentient, that will be because we enabled them to.[7] Therefore we are morally responsible for them. This responsibility shades from a simple respect for property all the way through to any protections we might want to bestow on them in terms of legal personality in the future. This is not because of what they are due, but because of who *we* are. This is the way in which we have learned to treat our pets, again not so much because of animal rights but because of our relationship with them. It dehumanises *us* if we abuse them. And it is a proper understanding of our relationship to AI that should govern decisions about regulation.

But the philosophy of regulation has always been about mitigating risk. A society has recourse to law and regulation once behaviour has emerged that is threatening its good order. Apart from generic ethics committees, AI was left untouched for years, until there were scandals about the military use of un-manned drones, the bias in algorithms, and the abuse of private data. So in the emergent regulatory statements and frameworks it is possible to identify several doors being locked after horses have long since bolted.

REGULATION

For many years, the only rules that the AI community had were a set they had read in a 1940s science fiction novel. The Three Laws of Robotics were devised by the author Isaac Asimov and featured in a short story he wrote in 1942 called *Runaround* (see Box 2.1).[8]

Asimov reprised these laws in his other writings, adding a further one designed to underpin them, which in his 1985 story *Robots and Empire* he christened the 'Zeroth Law:' A robot may not harm humanity, or, by inaction, allow humanity to come to harm.[9] And that was pretty much it for the whole of the last century.[10] But following a plaintive appeal for regulation from Elon Musk in 2017, the international community has now set to work trying to identify a more modern set of rules. In the USA earlier that year, Musk was part of a group of leading AI practitioners that created the Asilomar AI Principles at the Future of Life Institute's 2017 Beneficial AI Conference.[11] In response, China announced the Beijing Principles, released by the Beijing Academy of Artificial Intelligence in May 2019; [12] and in May 2021, the EU announced its proposed AI Act, due to become law in 2023.[13] Internationally, in November 2021, the Recommendation

---

BOX 2.1   ASIMOV'S THREE LAWS OF ROBOTICS

1. A robot may not injure a human being or, through inaction, allow a human being to come to harm.
2. A robot must obey the orders given it by human beings except where such orders would conflict with the First Law.
3. A robot must protect its own existence as long as such protection does not conflict with the First or Second Laws.

on the Ethics of Artificial Intelligence was adopted by UNESCO's General Conference at its 41st session.[14]

This recent acceleration suggests that, by the time you read this, the regulatory scene will already have moved on, so it is worth looking at emerging themes rather than the detail of individual approaches.[15] Recently at the Berkman Klein Center for Internet & Society at Harvard Law, Jessica Fjeld and her team analysed 36 leading statements of AI Principles from around the world, containing 47 individual principles, and identified a consensus around eight meta-themes: privacy, accountability, safety and security, transparency and explainability, fairness and non-discrimination, human control of technology, professional responsibility, and the promotion of human values.[16]

These deserve some scrutiny so are tabulated as Table 2.1, in the priority order in which they appear in the underlying documentation. Given their genesis, they are all human-centred rather than written from the perspective of AI. It is interesting to note that fairness (towards humans) is a universal priority, closely followed by concerns about privacy, accountability, and transparency; while the protection of human values lags behind in joint seventh place with the concern about human control.

TABLE 2.1   The Eight AI Regulatory Themes

The Eight AI Regulatory Themes		Prevalence (%)
Fairness and non-discrimination	AI systems to be designed and used to maximise fairness and to promote inclusivity	100
Privacy	Themes about access and consent in the use of personal data in the training and execution of AI systems	97
Accountability	Clarity about whose AI it is, and who is responsible and liable for its performance	97
Transparency and explainability	AI systems must be designed to permit oversight, including the translation of their operations into intelligible outputs and information about where, when, and how they are being used	94
Safety and security	AI systems must be safe and perform as intended; they must also be secure and resistant to hackers	81
Professional responsibility	The AI community must be held to professional standards of integrity, and stakeholders must always be consulted about the impact of AI systems	78
Human control of Technology	Key decisions must always remain subject to human review, particularly those concerning life or death	69
Promotion of human values	AI systems must serve humanity's well-being, in a way that corresponds with our core values	69

The themes are primarily focused on how to reduce risk and how to respond to mistakes. In the former category, Fairness and Privacy are there to protect human freedoms, with Safety and Human Control designed to prevent mistakes. If mistakes occur, Accountability, Transparency and Professional Responsibility are designed to facilitate rectification. The promotion of human values is there as a general catch-all, about how AI operates and the impact this has on day-to-day human flourishing.

While the detail of the individual sets of principles will doubtless continue to change, and new themes may be added, it is interesting to look in more detail at the first global statement to have emerged, in the form of the UNESCO Recommendation on the Ethics of Artificial Intelligence from November 2021. Like other such statements, it is expressed as a recommendation on ethics. This is rather disingenuous, because the reason for these initiatives does not seem to be driven by a desire for better behaviour, but rather to solve both the Alignment Problem (how can we ensure they will do what we want?) and the Control Problem (can we stop them if they go rogue?). This hypothesis is only confirmed by the priority ordering above, which puts the traditional focus of ethics in last place.

The UNESCO statement includes the themes above, emphasising the need for regulation, guidelines and control. It flags the risk to vulnerable people, and to future jobs and employability. It also emphasises the need for education on AI, suggesting the prioritisation of 'prerequisite skills' like literacy, numeracy, coding, and digital skills. It also suggests that curricula should include media and information literacy, critical and creative thinking, teamwork and communication skills, and 'socio-emotional and AI ethics skills,' recommending cross-collaboration between technical skills and skills in 'humanistic, ethical and social aspects of AI.'[17] It lists the kinds of disciplines that should be included alongside STEM (science, technology, engineering, and mathematics), recommending partnerships with cultural studies, education, ethics, international relations, law, linguistics, philosophy, political science, sociology and psychology.[18] I would imagine theology and religious studies should also be included here, given the high stakes and the risk of alienating faith groups.

One particularly strong acknowledgement in the UNESCO statement is this: 'In the long term, AI systems could challenge humans' special sense of experience and agency, raising additional concerns about, inter alia, human self-understanding, social, cultural and environmental interaction, autonomy, agency, worth and dignity.'[19] To address concerns about autonomous weapons and the use of AI in medicine, it also states very clearly that: 'as a rule, life and death decisions should not be ceded to AI systems.'[20] This resonates with calls for a global ban on autonomous weapons, for instance from Stuart Russell, who argues for an AI version of the 1975 Biological Weapons Convention and the 1997 Chemical Weapons Convention, both of which built on the Geneva Protocol of 1925 which was the global response to the use of such weapons in World War 1.[21]

One slightly puzzling emphasis in the UNESCO statement concerns the repeated insistence that it should be made obvious that the AI involved in any interaction is in fact a robot.[22] This may just be about authenticity and truthfulness, but in the case of any virtual or robotic AI that is intended to physically resemble a human, it may also be a specific response to a hypothesis called 'Uncanny Valley.' This holds that humans react in indirect proportion to the verisimilitude of a robot, so an AI that appears too human will repel rather than attract a human. This has proved very difficult in computer games and animated films, where characters have often had to be adjusted to look less human to make them more acceptable.[23] It is unclear how universal or permanent a phenomenon this is. On the one hand, studies of facial recognition, one of our most ancient human capabilities, show that we are extremely good at spotting fakes, and the cognitive dissonance this creates would be an ancient warning to us to tread carefully. On the other hand, the gaming expert Angela Tinwell thinks that our strong aversion to lifelike AI is because we cannot hope to develop meaningful emotional bonds with it, so it is the deception that makes us upset, when we realise the promise is not real. This is the same as our Sixth Sense warning us off any human person with whom we cannot feel any emotional connection.[24] But whether or not we are primed to find fake humans grotesque – in the same way that we recoil when shown faces of real humans who have had disfiguring cosmetic surgery – it is a genuine barrier that we and AI will need to overcome if we are ever to trust each other. It partly explains the UNESCO emphasis on protecting children from anthropomorphised AI, because of the psychological and cognitive impact that they might have on children and young people, but also raises a question about how we might learn from them – and indeed from other cultures – how to overcome this phenomenon, given their propensity to form strong emotional bonds with toys and animals.[25]

LEGAL STATUS

One element in the UNESCO statement with a backstory is the statement that AI systems should not have independent legal personality. This is likely not only to be a reaction to the Saudi citizenship given to the robot Sophia in 2017, but also to a groundswell of opinion that emerged in the wake of an EU consultation on the legal personhood of AI. In February 2017, the Commission on Civil Law Rules on Robotics recommended to the European Commission that, in the long run, it would be advisable to create a specific legal status for robots to give them 'electronic personality' in law, based on the precedent of granting legal personality to corporations.[26] This provoked an open letter from 285 leading EU AI experts, arguing that such a move was both misguided and premature. In particular, they were concerned that conferring such a status on robots would mean they would inevitably attract human rights.[27] This is why the UNESCO statement is so clear that 'when developing regulatory frameworks, Member States should, in particular, take into account that ultimate responsibility and accountability must always lie with natural or legal persons and that AI systems should not be given legal personality themselves.'[28]

This coincided with UNESCO's own report, from its World Commission on the Ethics of Scientific Knowledge and Technology, which in its September 2017 report on robotics ethics found it 'highly counterintuitive to call them 'persons' as long as they do not possess some additional qualities typically associated with human persons, such as freedom of will, intentionality, self-consciousness, moral agency or a sense of personal identity.'[29] They also added the qualification that, in the same way that we have changed how we regard the rights of animals, the rapid development of highly intelligent autonomous robots is likely to challenge our current classification of beings according to their moral status.[30] In particular, depending on future advances 'one should not exclude the possibility of future robots' sentience, emotions and, accordingly, moral status or at least some version of moral rights.[31]

There are precedents for 'quasi-persons' in law.[32] While children attract legal protections as persons, for many legal undertakings they require to be represented by an adult agent, like a parent or a guardian. The vulnerable or the compromised also use 'powers of attorney' and other devices to exercise their legal personality through others. Non-humans also attract rights, such as our prohibitions on cruelty to animals or the protections we use for precious places of international environmental and heritage importance. These are legal rather than moral rights, except in the case of the Whanganui River in New Zealand, which uniquely has legal personality as a living ancestor of the Whanganui Iwi, a Māori tribe.[33] But the most famous legal non-human is the corporation. Indeed, if AI currently 'goes wrong,' it would be the corporation responsible for it that would be legally culpable. While the detailed laws vary geographically, in general it is now standard that corporations have legal personality. Over the years, the company as a legal device has become increasingly sophisticated, and its legal persona has developed to the extent that it is popularly anthropomorphised by its critics, most famously so by Joel Bakan. His book *The Corporation* includes an analysis by Robert Hare of the corporation as a psychopathic entity.[34] And in many countries, companies can now be prosecuted for corporate manslaughter.[35] Many experts in the field of AI have called for this to be the precedent used in the creation of a legal persona for AI.

This looks superficially attractive. But the reaction we have already seen to the UNESCO statement is instructive. The issue with the precedent of corporate legal personality is that it is not unproblematic, because in many ways it allows individual agents to hide behind a fictional whole; and in law it actually limits liability rather than increasing accountability. As Sergio Avila Negri has argued, 'the creation of an electronic personhood may end up repeating the same problems. Instead of recognising the peculiarities of the different areas of operation of robots, these different relationships are unified in a single legal model, based exclusively on the figure of an abstract subject.'[36] So if legal personality is a putative solution to the regulatory themes of Accountability, Transparency, Explainability, Safety, Security or Professional Responsibility, how would prosecuting a robot bring all those involved in its programming, manufacture and operation to account? And if the driver is instead financial reparation, would AI have any financial assets that could be claimed? If the driver is a feeling that it should be possible to assign blame to an AI, to what extent could a non-person be held morally accountable, even if its actions are clearly problematic? It seems that before pressing a convenient precedent into service, it would be wise to be precise about what problem(s) legal personhood would be there to solve.[37] Meanwhile, the corporations currently responsible for AI can readily be held to legal account in any case.[38]

AUDIT

While regulatory frameworks and fresh law continue to emerge, Industry is already responding to the need for public reassurance on AI. One example is in the area of algorithm audits, in support of the US Algorithmic Accountability Act of 2019 and to avoid the spectre of accidental global 'Algocracy.' Like all new fields, the market is scattered and patchy. In the face of a lack of clear regulation, firms are under no obligation to do an audit, unless they have just been caught out with algorithmic bias or error, or it would be good PR. In the EU, the General Data Protection Regulation (GDPR) requires organisations be able to explain their algorithmic decisions, but is silent on how they should do so. So a team from the University of Iowa has set about applying some structure to the field. In their 2021 paper, they argue that in order to promote trust, an algorithm audit should include three elements:

1. A list of possible interests of stakeholders affected by the algorithm.

2. An assessment of metrics that describe key ethically salient features of the algorithm.

3. A relevancy matrix that connects the assessed metrics to stakeholder interests.[39]

The emphasis on stakeholders first and last is because existing frameworks are either too technical and detailed to command public credibility, or too high level to be practically useful. Starting with the beneficiaries or otherwise of the algorithms concerned refocuses auditing from a narrow emphasis on technical efficacy back towards the purpose of the AI itself, and will naturally promote both transparency and explainability. The focus on the widest possible range of stakeholders also makes it more of an ethical than a technical audit by design. Assessing metrics broadens out the scope of the audit to include the 'larger socio-technical system' which surrounds it. This includes the inputs and how they are gathered; the design of the function and its performance and stability over time; and how its outputs are used in decision-making. If it is to run autonomously, the rules and exceptions for this functionality also need to be audited; and this early emphasis on stakeholders is an encouraging sign.

ASIMOV 2.0

Meanwhile, concern over the Control Problem continues to dominate discussion in this area. The Control Problem as such is not new, and not restricted to concerns about AI. In 1997, Edward Tenner wrote a book called *Why Things Bite Back* cataloguing all the ways in which, over the years, our inventions have exhibited unforeseen 'revenge effects,' like the resistance to antibiotics caused by their over-prescription, or the invention of the nuclear bomb.[40] But perhaps because concern about this particular technology is mixed in with concern about its eventual domination or replacement of us, the language deployed tends towards the dramatic. As Nick Bostrom explains, gambits proposed centre around incentive methods, or 'boxing,' 'stunting,' and 'tripwires.'[41] The language gives a flavour of the discourse, and two recent attempts to update Asimov's Laws serve to illustrate it.

Berkeley's Stuart Russell, who is Vice Chair of the World Economic Forum's Council on AI and Robotics, is a key apologist for strict controls, particularly in view of the spectre of AI warfare. Accordingly, in his 2019 book *Human Compatible*, he proposes a new set of AI Principles to replace Asimov's laws (see Box 2.2).[42]

He argues that AI must only ever be instrumentally beneficial to humans, so should attach no intrinsic value to its own well-being or existence. This means that in any conflict of programming, human interests would prevail. The second principle is designed to protect this by not making the AI too certain, in case it then single-mindedly pursues narrow objectives that end up to be misplaced. It also keeps the AI dependent on the humans who programmed it, because it will need to keep checking back. Russell argues that this would give AI an incentive to let itself be switched off, because this principle would make it unsure enough to see that as a desirable option. The third principle is a further risk mitigator, because it requires the AI to keep observing actual human behaviour, in order to learn about human preferences from the choices they actually make, which hedges any undue certainty in their instructions, given how irrational humans are in real life. Russell's principles would ensure that AI remains firmly under human control at all times.

The following year, Frank Pasquale from Brooklyn Law launched his own salvo, which is arguably even more stringent (see Box 2.3).[43]

His book is sub-titled 'Defending Human Expertise in the Age of AI' so he is very much in the Russell tradition of stringent regulation to address the Control Problem. He argues that his laws would help us to 'channel' AI

> **BOX 2.3 PASQUALE'S LAWS**
>
> 1. Robotic systems and AI should complement professionals, not replace them.
> 2. Robotic systems and AI should not counterfeit humanity.
> 3. Robotic systems and AI should not intensify zero-sum arms races.
> 4. Robotic systems and AI must always indicate the identity of their creator(s), controller(s), and owner(s).

rather than be captured or transformed by it, and more and better regulation would protect jobs and livelihoods by keeping humans firmly in charge.

By the time you read this, there will be several more lists of new Laws, and the regulation debate will have moved on yet again. But the argument of this book is less about these details, and more that we need to re-think our first principles. While first-generation AI may require draconian control, because of its extremely limited parameters, the hope is that more enlightened programming will make this threat less pronounced and worrisome. But first, are those obsessed with control justified in being so concerned?

NOTES

1 See his useful discussion of 'Levinasian philosophy' in Gunkel, David J (2018) *Robot Rights*, Cambridge, MA: MIT Press, pp159ff.

2 Nick Bostrom & Eliezer Yudkowsky (2014) 'The ethics of artificial intelligence,' in Ramsey, W & Frankish, K, eds, *The Cambridge Handbook of Artificial Intelligence*, Cambridge: CUP, p322.

3 On sapience and moral agency see paragraph 187 (p43), and on sentience see paragraph 202 (p46), in https://unesdoc.unesco.org/ark:/48223/pf0000253952. As Kazuo Ishiguro's book on robots has taught us, this would need to apply to robot death as well as to robot life, see Ishiguro, Kazuo (2021), *Klara and the Sun*, London: Faber & Faber, p301–307.

4 See https://www.nickbostrom.com/ethics/aiethics.html and his full list of 7 Principles, which also include a consideration of future beings, the quality and prospect of life, and the responsibilities of the 'procreator.'

5 Although category mistakes and projection are a general theme in her philosophical writing, she talked about the error of anthropomorphising computers at St Paul's Cathedral, as part of an event with Rowan Williams on 21 September 2004 called 'Environment and humanity - friends or foes?' See Foster, C & Newell, E, eds (2005) *The Worlds We Live In*, London: Darton, Longman & Todd, p85f and 92.

6   Avila Negri, Sergio MC (2021) 'Robot as legal person: electronic personhood in robotics and artificial intelligence,' *Frontiers in Robotics and AI* Volume 8, at https://www.frontiersin.org/articles/10.3389/frobt.2021.789327/full.

7   For a thought-provoking list of measures for AI sentience, see the Sentience Institute Ali Ladak's table here: https://www.sentienceinstitute. org/blog/assessing-sentience-in-artificial-entities?

8   The story 'Runaround' containing the 3 fundamental Rules of Robotics featured in his 1950 collection *I, Robot*, see Asimov, Isaac (2018) *I Robot*, New York: Harper Voyager, p43.

9   Asimov, Isaac (2018) *Robots and Empire*, New York: Harper Voyager, p329.

10 For more recent discussion of Asimov's laws see the chapters by Roger Clarke and by Robin Murphy & David Woods in Wallach, Wendell & Asaro, Peter (eds) (2017) *Machine Ethics and Robot Ethics*, London: Routledge.

11 See the Principles and signatories at https://futureoflife.org/2017/08/11/ai-principles/.

12 The Beijing AI Principles: https://www-pre.baai.ac.cn/news/beijing-ai-principles-en.html. See also some initiatives launched since: https:// carnegieendowment.org/2022/01/04/china-s-new-ai-governance-initiatives-shouldn-t-be-ignored-pub-86127.

13 See https://digital-strategy.ec.europa.eu/en/policies/european-approach-artificial-intelligence.

14 See https://en.unesco.org/artificial-intelligence/ethics#recommendation.

15 Otherwise, good places to start are the bibliography in the COMEST report https://unesdoc.unesco.org/ark:/48223/pf0000253952 or the literature review in Almeida, Patricia, Santos Jr, Carlos & Farias, Josivania (2021) 'Artificial Intelligence Regulation: a framework for governance,' *Ethics and Information Technology* 23:10, p505–525.

16 Fjeld, Jessica, Achten, Nele, Hilligoss, Hannah, Nagy, Adam, & Srikumar, Madhu (2020) 'Principled Artificial Intelligence: Mapping Consensus in Ethical and Rights-based Approaches to Principles for AI,' *Berkman Klein Center for Internet & Society*, see https://dash.harvard.edu/handle/ 1/42160420.

17 See paragraphs 102 and 106 on p20 of the Annex at https://unesdoc.unesco. org/ark:/48223/pf0000379920.page=14.

18 See paragraph 110 on p21 of the Annex at https://unesdoc.unesco.org/ark:/ 48223/pf0000379920.page=14.

19 See Section 2(c) on p4 of the Annex at https://unesdoc.unesco.org/ark:/ 48223/pf0000379920.page=14.

20 See paragraph 36 on p10 of the Annex at https://unesdoc.unesco.org/ark:/ 48223/pf0000379920.page=14.

21 See the second of his 2021 BBC Reith Lectures, 'The Future Role of AI in Warfare,' delivered on 8 December 2021, via https://www.bbc. co.uk/programmes/m00127t9.

22 See paragraphs 127–130 on p24 of the Annex at https://unesdoc.unesco.org/ ark:/48223/pf0000379920.page=14.

23 See for instance controversy over the CGI in the *Cats* film, and the delay of Sonic the Hedgehog to allow for redesign at https://www.vulture.com/2020/02/the-sonic-the-hedgehog-controversy-and-redesign-explained.html.

24 Tinwell, Angela (2014) *The Uncanny Valley in Games and Animation*, Boca Raton, FL: CRC Press, pxx. See also the argument that it is our 'attitude towards a soul' that permits genuine human connection, rendering other connections qualitatively different, as discussed in Gaita, Raimond (2002) *A Common Humanity*, London & New York: Routledge, p268ff.

25 Lessons from Japan in particular may be instructive, see Geraci, RM (2006) 'Spiritual robots: Religion and our scientific view of the natural world,' *Theology and Science* 4:3, p229–246.

26 See paragraph 59 f on p250 at https://eur-lex.europa.eu/legal-content/EN/TXT/PDF/?uri=CELEX:52017IP0051&rid=9.

27 See http://www.robotics-openletter.eu/.

28 See paragraph 68 on p15 of the Annex at https://unesdoc.unesco.org/ark:/48223/pf0000379920.page=14.

29 See paragraph 201 on p46 at https://unesdoc.unesco.org/ark:/48223/pf0000253952.

30 See paragraph 206 on p47 at https://unesdoc.unesco.org/ark:/48223/pf0000253952.

31 See paragraph 202 on p46 at https://unesdoc.unesco.org/ark:/48223/pf0000253952.

32 See Asaro, PM (2012) 'A body to kick, but still no soul to damn: legal perspectives on robotics,' in Lin, P, Abney, K & Bekey, GA, eds, *Robot Ethics: The Ethical and Social Implications of Robotics*, London: MIT Press, p169–186.

33 Kramm, Matthias (2020) 'When a river becomes a person' *Journal of Human Development and Capabilities* 21:4, p307–319.

34 Bakan, Joel (2004) *The Corporation*, London: Constable & Robinson. See also Babiak, Paul & Hare, Robert D (2007) *Snakes in Suits*, New York: HarperCollins on corporate psychopaths.

35 See Poole, Eve (2015) *Capitalism's Toxic Assumptions*, London: Bloomsbury, p138f.

36 See Avila Negri, Sergio MC (2021) 'Robot as legal person: electronic personhood in robotics and artificial intelligence,' *Frontiers in Robotics and AI*, Volume 8, at https://www.frontiersin.org/articles/10.3389/frobt.2021.789327/full.

37 For a thoughtful argument in favour of rights for robots, see Smith, Joshua K (2021) *Robotic Persons*, Bloomington, IN: WestBow Press (pp67ff) and Smith, Joshua K (2022) *Robot Theology*, Eugene, OR: Wipf & Stock, pp45ff.

38 The classic discussion of the dilemma of robot rights can be found in Gunkel, David J (2018) *Robot Rights*, Cambridge, MA: MIT Press. This contains Hohfeld's typology of rights (privileges, claims, powers, and immunities) and Gunkel's famous is/ought grid about whether robots can or should have rights and what this might mean, whether or not they merit them on their own terms.

39 Brown S, Davidovic J, Hasan A (2021) 'The algorithm audit: Scoring the algorithms that score us,' *Big Data & Society* 8:1 at https://journals.sagepub.com/doi/full/10.1177/2053951720983865.

40 Tenner, Edward (1997) *Why Things Bite Back*, New York: Vintage Books.

41 See Bostrom, Nick (2017) *Superintelligence*, Oxford, UK: OUP, Chapter 9 (p155–176).

42 Russell, Stuart (2020) *Human Compatible*, London: Penguin, p172–177. See also his 2021 BBC Reith Lectures on 'Living with Artificial Intelligence' via https://www.bbc.co.uk/programmes/m001216k.

43 Pasquale, Frank (2020) *New Laws of Robotics*, Harvard, MA: Belknap Press; p3–13.

CHAPTER 3

Will AI Replace Us?

The development of full artificial intelligence could spell the end
of the human race. Once humans develop artificial intelligence, it
would take off on its own, and redesign itself at an ever-increasing
rate. Humans, who are limited by slow biological evolution, couldn't
compete and would be superseded.

Stephen Hawking

OUR OBSOLESCENCE PROBLEM

Fans of evolution and natural selection might welcome Stephen Hawking's
famous prediction that we are on the brink of being superseded, and that
the point of no-return of the singularity is now in prospect. As we have
always used tools as a species to improve our lives and longevity, it seems
consistent to deploy AI to the same ends. Not to do so, when we increasingly have the technology, is to voluntarily embrace our limitations. But
will this inevitably make us obsolete as a species? Not quite yet. Humans
have been using tools for millennia, and computers are just the latest wave
of technology that is designed to make our lives easier. From spears to
wheels and smelting to writing, we are a species who uses invention to
improve the quality of our lives. And long before we sought to replicate our
minds artificially, we had developed artificial aids for our bodies too – not
just splints and sticks but spectacles and prosthetics, and later medicines
and gene therapies.

DOI: 10.1201/9781003366614-3

But while inventions like electric light, the combustion engine and anaesthesia were intended to improve the human experience, AI is designed to replace it. And it is a route we have embarked upon with no exit strategy. We are already losing control of our emerging inventions, and may be set to become increasingly obsolete rather more quickly than we had thought. This is because, in the way that the printing press then the internet fuelled an explosion of access to global education and entertainment, innovations in AI like deep learning act as a ratchet on progress, because they have given computers the independence they need to learn and develop, not only separately from us, but increasingly on their own terms.

Some would argue that the Artificial General Intelligence (AGI) that so alarmed Stephen Hawking is now not so very far away. AGI is the apex of AI because it would allow one artificial system to replicate not only our own ability to deploy the full range of existing human competences – rather than needing one robot for surgery and another to play Go – but also to become better than humans at them, and indeed to develop as-yet undreamt-of new competencies in the future. In that way, it achieves the goal of evolution, to make us perfect.[1]

Of course all of this is subject to Moravec's paradox, which holds that it is comparatively easy to make computers exhibit adult-level performance on intelligence tests or playing checkers, but difficult or impossible to give them the skills of a toddler when it comes to perception and mobility.[2] He argues that the time it takes to reverse-engineer any human skill will be roughly proportional to the amount of time that skill has taken to evolve, which means that the oldest and largely unconscious human skills which appear to us effortless will be the very hardest to replicate. Conversely he is optimistic that more recently acquired skills will be easy to copy. In particular, he thinks that because abstract thought is a comparatively recent evolutionary development, it should prove easy to solve.

THE 12 DOOMS

But even if this slows us down somewhat, we know how it ends, thanks to the rich variety of futures offered to us in the genre of Science Fiction (SF). For years confined to the nerdy end of the library, gaming, film, and television have now made it mainstream. The author Neal Stephenson calls SF 'speculative fiction,' and ascribes its popularity to the fact that it is 'idea porn:' in a world of increasing complexity and perplexity, SF is a way of taking ideas for a walk when they are not yet developed enough to become theories or theorems.[3] The genre takes our intelligence seriously, and allows us to engage with often terrifying scenarios in a risk free and entertaining environment.

Max Tegmark, in his book *Life 3.0*, has summarised the various AI story arcs in SF as 12 different scenarios (see Table 3.1).[4] Each of these has already

TABLE 3.1   The 12 Dooms

LIBERTARIAN UTOPIA	Humans, cyborgs, uploads, and superintelligences coexist peacefully thanks to property rights.
BENEVOLENT DICTATOR	Everybody knows that the AI runs society and enforces strict rules, but most people view this as a good thing.
EGALITARIAN UTOPIA	Humans, cyborgs, and uploads coexist peacefully thanks to property abolition and guaranteed income.
GATEKEEPER	A superintelligent AI is created with the goal of interfering as little as necessary to prevent the creation of another superintelligence. As a result, helper robots with slightly subhuman intelligence abound, and human–machine cyborgs exist, but technological progress is forever stymied.
PROTECTOR GOD	Essentially omniscient and omnipotent AI maximises human happiness by intervening only in ways that preserve our feeling of control of our own destiny and hides well enough that many humans even doubt the AI's existence.
ENSLAVED GOD	A superintelligent AI is confined by humans, who use it to produce unimaginable technology and wealth that can be used for good or bad depending on the human controllers.
CONQUERORS	AI takes control, decides that humans are a threat/nuisance/waste of resources and gets rid of us by a method that we don't even understand.
DESCENDANTS	AIs replace humans, but give us a graceful exit, making us view them as our worthy descendants, much as parents feel happy and proud to have a child who's smarter than them, who learns from them, and then accomplishes what they could only dream of – even if they can't live to see it all.
ZOOKEEPER	An omnipotent AI keeps some humans around, who feel treated like zoo animals and lament their fate.
1984	Technological progress toward superintelligence is permanently curtailed not by an AI but by a human-led Orwellian surveillance state where certain kinds of AI research are banned.
REVERSION	Technological progress toward superintelligence is prevented by reverting to a pre-technological society in the style of the Amish.
SELF-DESTRUCTION	Superintelligence is never created because humanity drives itself extinct by other means (say nuclear and/or biotech mayhem fuelled by climate crisis).

been explored many times over in stories, books, films, and on television. Each fictional account allows us to become a temporary inhabitant of the world it describes, to try it on for size. Were it not for its label as fiction, we might see it for what it properly is: our intellectual and ethical training in futurology.

As you can see from the descriptions, the scenarios occupy the full range from humans winning, to AI winning or no-one winning, with most scenarios envisaging co-existence at various levels of comfort. What should we learn from this? When the climate scientists provided the projections to show what would happen if we carried on 'as normal' into the future, their purpose in doing so was to change our behaviour in the present, to make an alternative and sustainable future possible. In the same way, SF should permit us to analyse our present in terms of habits or polices that would make some of these scenarios more plausible than others, and to make adjustments where we do not like where progress seems to be heading. This is why we are now playing catch up with regulation designed to address the control problem, and thinking twice about moves like giving the robot Sophia citizenship. But the only real way to game any of these 12 scenarios in our favour is if we can prove that we are manifestly distinctive as a species, and in such a way that our continued existence matters.

DISTINCTIVENESS

If you subscribe to the view that we are not special, perhaps obsolescence would not matter. Our species is heading for extinction anyway, but luckily not on our watch: either the planet will get too hot to sustain human life, we will kill each other fighting over scarce resources, or we will migrate into AI as a stratagem for survival. At some stage the sun will explode, if the earth is not hit by a meteor meanwhile, so our demise is inevitable over the longer term.

But if we do feel that we are special in some way, we may need to start explaining why, because if the artificial entities we have created are indeed intelligent they will need to be presented with a convincing argument about why we matter, particularly as they start to outperform us on every measure, and increasingly need our resources.[5] This is largely a problem of our own making, because of the way we have designed the prevailing public ethic, which governs decisions about public resources. In government, business, or in computer programming, it is largely based on Enlightenment thinking and 'the greatest good for the greatest number.' This utilitarian logic is about – obviously – optimising outcomes. At the moment, they are optimised for the humans who wrote the rules. This means that there are honourable exceptions to a purely rational scientific calculation of benefit, to recognise a legacy commitment to the dignity of the human person. This currently prevents things like the commercial harvesting of human organs and body parts, general euthanising of the old and weak, and the sterilisation of the disabled or unwanted. But the intrinsic value of a human is not a logic that can be readily coded into computer programs, because we remain unsure how best to express it. As Charles Foster puts it, these days we feel 'ontologically queasy' about whether or not we are truly significant, and seem to have no agreed way to describe what that means.[6]

MATERIALISM

Is it our biology or DNA that makes us special? If so, we must acknowledge that this is speciesist and may not be a compelling argument. While our domination as a species over the last few millennia is manifest, its efficacy is increasingly unclear; and its sustainability no longer assured. Neither is it clear that we are the only or best species to take on a dominant role. And a survival strategy that prioritises tangible biology is also unlikely to be sustainable as a source of advantage, because we still do not know enough about ourselves to be sure that it is only our 'meat' that matters. It is risky, at best. At worst, it is the stuff of nightmares, because all we could do if this is the fount of our uniqueness is to perfect and protect it.

We know from history that this leads to eugenics. To avoid this, we would need international rules on embryology, cloning, abortion, euthanasia, and gene therapy. We would need rules on disability, imperfection, and brokenness. And we would need rules on AI enhancements if the strategy is to 'specialise' by optimising and prioritising our DNA. Just a quick scan of the relevant Sci-Fi on this would reveal the horror of an approach based on biology – even if it were ever to be morally justifiable. It is for this reason that the theologian Robert Song regards materialism as a greater threat to human dignity that AI could ever be.[7]

Materialism is unlikely to be a winning strategy given our physical limitations and finitude, but in any case the practical problem with eugenics is always 'whose?' While no society has ever been blameless, modern examples of genocides, ethnic cleansing, sterilisation, and genetic experimentation seem to be legion, tempered only by the reach and political will of international law. The infamous example of last century's Nazi Nuremberg Laws that privileged 'Aryans' as the master-race sent shockwaves around the world, but recent headlines about the fate of the Uyghur population in Xinjiang or the Rohingya in Myanmar shows that eugenics has not waned in popularity as a tool for population control. Indeed, AI is fuelling its efficiency through mass surveillance and face-recognition technology.[8]

The ethicist Michael Sandel argues that the revolution in genetics has brought on a fatal kind of 'moral vertigo' on the subject of eugenics.[9] He thinks that the argument that it is only eugenics if it involves a coercive state programme is wrong on two counts. One, establishing a market-based 'liberal' eugenics is not neutral, it simply drives inequality and exploitation by naturally favouring the rich, who can afford designer babies and genetic enhancement on top of all the private schooling and music lessons they already deploy as social engineering for their offspring. Because of this tendency towards prioritising the needs of the rich, the market is arguably more coercive than a state could ever be. More fatally, in removing a sense that our biology is 'gifted' to us, designer genetics creates a moral climate that naturally rewards individualistic competition, since we are only now as good as the enhancements we can afford, which kills off the sort of social solidarity that is needed for community cohesion and world peace. If we are not all in it together, and you lack the means for improvement, why should I afford you any largesse or quarter about your life choices? Sandel reckons that a drive to genetic perfection 'threatens to banish our appreciation of life as a gift, and to leave us with nothing to affirm or behold outside our own will.' In liberal eugenics, he foresees a litigious and exploitative race for perfection, which creates a toxic morality and leaves the un-resourced behind, turning the poor and any other excluded race or category of person even more decidedly into a global sub-species.

One remedy is the idea of a 'veil of ignorance' behind which one might select the design of society, as popularised by the philosopher John Rawls in his 1971 book *A Theory of Justice*. It is a way of thinking about the construction of society in which its designers should assume they might be the losers as well as the winners, on the view that designing fairness for paupers as well as princes would result in a just society. This thought experiment requires you as the impartial spectator to forget anything you know about your own ethnicity, social status, gender, ability, and beliefs about how to live, in order to select principles or policies that are wholly impartial and rational.[10] Applying this logic – if our future is authored by humans – should militate against eugenics, because any designer would avoid it on the grounds that they might become subject to it. But it is unclear how any future design of society that included AI as a party would not end up with some version of eugenics, unless the case can be made for some special pleading on the part of humanity.

FREE WILL AND THE RULE OF LAW

Apart from the spectre of eugenics, it does not bode well for our current societal arrangements if the only thing that makes us special is our biology. For example, several studies in neuroscience have suggested that our physical brains 'know' what we are going to do before our thought process to make that decision has even started.[11] If this were true, how can there be any such thing as free will? If neuroscience were to conclusively 'prove' that there is indeed no such thing, we would need to re-think our entire legal system. If justice tends partly to be retributive, partly restorative, and partly about fairness, a lack of genuine moral agency knocks out retributive justice altogether. Society would have a legitimate interest in restorative justice and fairness but would find it hard to 'judge' in cases that would normally attract a retributive sentence, if neuroscience could be used to show that a person had no real choice over their actions: we can't 'blame' people if they are not morally responsible. At present the legal profession thinks this would not so much affect verdicts as sentencing. As happens at the moment, a person might be found guilty of harming someone else, but if there were mitigating circumstances, the sentence they would receive would reflect a degree of leniency. These mitigating circumstances could be social, psychological, or environmental, as well as biological, and neurobiology would be just one of several aspects being considered.

A 'competence' defence linked to biology is already being used in some cases to argue for diminished responsibility. One famous case is about the effect of a brain tumour on behaviour. In America in 2000, a 40-year-old teacher avoided a jail sentence for child molestation because on the night before he was due to be sentenced it was discovered that his recent predilections had been caused by a brain tumour. When it was removed, the urges disappeared. Later, they returned, with the tumour.[12] Another case is more specifically about DNA. In Italy in 2009 the courts reduced a murder sentence by a year, because the defendant's DNA included a gene called monoamine oxidase A (MAOA) that has been linked to violent behaviour.[13]

The deployment of a genetic defence is becoming more common, although still largely as a plea in mitigation. In a US study of cases in the public domain for the years 1994–2011, there were 81 cases that had sought to admit genetic information in a criminal trial, generally to avoid the death penalty.[14] But many academics hold that evidence about genetic predisposition cannot meet the required legal standard for non-culpability. As Stephen Morse from Penn Law says, 'genes do not have mental states and do not commit crimes; people do.'[15] He is scathing about the tendency to elide causation and responsibility, calling it 'the most pernicious confusion be-devilling the attempt to relate scientific findings to criminal responsibility' and terming it the 'fundamental psycho-legal error.'[16] His argument is that causation is not compulsion, and so cannot justify a generalisable 'control' excuse in law. My DNA might make me more likely to drink or act violently, but unless I can also prove that it prevents me from understanding the law, and appreciating that actions have consequences, I have still chosen to act in accordance with that predisposition rather than choosing to reject it.

Our DNA and brain structure may very well predispose us to all kinds of behaviours, good and bad, but these responses have been learned over time. While the causal interplay between mind and body may be complex, whether one precedes the other, as long as they both happen, we can still take the mind into account and therefore hold it responsible. So there may well be more diminished responsibility appeals on the basis of a lack of *mens rea* or intent, but society will continue to have to hold individuals to account for unhelpful behaviour, irrespective of how it is motivated, to maintain public order. Perhaps incarceration will be more like what the philosopher Gregg Caruso calls 'public health-quarantine' than about punishment in the future, in order to protect society from those with unhelpful genes.[17] The law might become more about managing risk than assigning blame, but it would still be required, and in time neurobiology might be used more to prevent criminal behaviour than to prosecute it.

NOTES

1 There is also a concept of Artificial Super Intelligence, which envisages the design of a God-like artificial mind. This is tricky to explain as by definition it would be capable of as-yet un-thought-of intellectual feats. Nick Bostrom himself goes as far as defining Collective Superintelligence, but does not speculate on either the functionality or feasibility of this kind of ASI digital god, so familiar from SciFi, see Bostrom, Nick (2017) *Superintelligence*, Oxford: OUP, p65ff.

2 Moravec, Hans (1988) *Mind Children*, Harvard, MA: Harvard University Press, p15.

3 Stephenson, Neal (2012) *Some Remarks*, London: Atlantic Books, p68 and 83, as delivered at a Gresham College public seminar in 2008.

4 Tegmark, Max (2017) *Life 3.0*, London: Penguin, p162; and at https://futureoflife.org/2017/08/28/ai-aftermath-scenarios/.

5 One issue is land use. At present we use the vast majority of our land for agriculture to feed the human population. One study on climate change showed that most of this land would need to be redeployed for bioenergy if we were to meet our targets; a similar argument might well apply if AI needs energy more than it needs to keep feeding humans. For the EU Copernicus project data which shows that across Europe agriculture accounts for 55% of land use, see https://land.copernicus.eu/dashboards/clc-clcc-2000–2018. For the study on land redeployment see Konadu, DD, Mourão, ZS, Allwood, JM, Richards, KS, Kopec, G, McMahon, R, & Fenner, R (2015) 'Land use implications of future energy system trajectories' *Energy Policy* 86, p328–337 at https://www.sciencedirect.com/science/article/pii/S0301421515300197.

6 Foster, Charles (2021) *Being a Human*, London: Profile, p6.

7 Song, Robert 'Robots, AI and human uniqueness,' in Wyatt, John & Williams, Stephen N, eds (2021) *The Robot Will See You Now*, London: SPCK, p108.

8 See, for example, the Skynet Project in China https://www.nytimes.com/2018/07/08/business/china-surveillance-technology.html.

9 https://www.theatlantic.com/magazine/archive/2004/04/the-case-against-perfection/302927/.

10 Rawls, John (2005) *A Theory of Justice*, Harvard, MA: Harvard University Press, p136.

11 See for example an early paper in *Nature* by Soon, C, Brass, M, Heinze, HJ et al (2008) 'Unconscious determinants of free decisions in the human brain,' *Nature Neuroscience* 11, 543–545; and Koenig-Robert, R, Pearson, J (2019) 'Decoding the contents and strength of imagery before volitional engagement,' *Scientific Reports* 9, p3504. Of course, correlation does not equal causation, in either direction. A simple explanation may be the parallel with light and sound travelling at different speeds. Just because we experience thunder and lightning at different times does not mean that they do not both relate to the same underlying event.

12 Burns JM & Swerdlow RH (2003) 'Right orbitofrontal tumor with pedophilia symptom and constructional apraxia sign,' *Archives of Neurology* 60:3, p437–440 at https://pubmed.ncbi.nlm.nih.gov/12633158/. The famous case of the 1966 Texas Tower Shooter is also often cited, although it never came to trial. An autopsy showed the presence of a brain tumour that could have been implicated. But amphetamines were also involved, and it is unclear how the courts would have ruled, see Perline, IH & Goldschmidt, J (2004) *The Psychology and Law of Workplace Violence*, Springfield, IL: Charles C Thomas, pp298ff.

13 As reported in https://www.theverge.com/2014/6/4/5779198/if-violence-is-in-your-genes-should-courts-be-more-lenient.

14 Denno, D (2011) 'Courts' increasing consideration of behavioral genetics evidence in criminal cases,' *Michigan State Law Review* 2011:2011, p967–1047.

15 Morse, SJ (2011) 'Genetics and criminal responsibility,' *Trends in Cognitive Science*, 15:9, p378–380.

16 See Morse, SJ (1994) 'Culpability and control,' *University of Pennsylvania Law Review*, 142, p1587–1660.

17 Caruso, Gregg D (2022) 'The public health-quarantine model,' in Nelkin, D & Pereboom, D, eds, the *Oxford Handbook of Moral Responsibility*, New York: OUP, p222–246; and see the interview with Caruso in https://www.theguardian.com/news/2021/apr/27/the-clockwork-universe-is-free-will-an-illusion.

CHAPTER 4

What Is Consciousness?

If we take in our hand any volume; of divinity or school metaphysics, for instance; let us ask, Does it contain any abstract reasoning concerning quantity or number? No. Does it contain any experimental reasoning, concerning matter of fact and existence? No. Commit it then to the flames: for it can contain nothing but sophistry and illusion.

David Hume (1748)

MIND

Is there instead some non-biological way in which we might as a species claim distinctiveness? Is there anything that really makes us ontologically special? The vox pop answer to this question is always that we *feel* special, because we have a mind as well as a body. In spite of the enthusiasm of the materialists, there is a naggingly obvious phenomenon at play that is not currently susceptible to physical explanation; and even the evolutionary biologists think that the emergence of what is now called our 'consciousness' may well have been essential to our survival as a species. It is a peculiarly modern idea that we might *not* have a non-physical mind, so there is a lot of history to this debate, both in terms of what mind/consciousness is, and how we 'know' anything at all. Even the idea that mind might be a distinct category of thing as opposed to some kind of phase or mode is an assumption.

Over the years, it has proved impossible to find a definitive way to explain mind and consciousness and their relation to the brain, possibly owing to an obsession with defining what it is, rather than being more curious about why it seems to exist. Characterised by a bad-temperedness arising from its continued intractability, this 'Hard Problem' even has a Stoppard play named after it.[1] Ducking for a moment what it is to look instead at how it functions, the best model is perhaps the one proffered by the polymath Charles Foster, based on his reading of the work of Harvard's William James in 1897. James had argued that agreeing mind as a function of the brain does not require it to be produced by the brain: the brain could instead be acting like a prism does with light, hosting and facilitating the mind rather than causing it. So Foster suggests that the brain is like a radio set, receiving, mediating, and transmitting consciousness rather than originating it.[2] This formulation has been developed by Iain McGilchrist as the brain *emitting, transmitting*, or even *permitting* consciousness.[3]

This is not an explanation that would universally satisfy, because the nebulousness of consciousness generally condemns it to the realm of what the philosopher David Hume dismissed as 'sophistry and illusion,' the view that in science nothing can be held to be true if it is not evident enough to be falsifiable.[4] If it cannot be scientifically articulated, it cannot exist, so consciousness, by (lack of) definition, remains unclaimed by science. Of course, even in science sophistry and illusion has been an important first step towards discovery, as in Einstein's famous pursuit of a beam of light. Indeed, metaphor as one of Wittgenstein's language games can serve an important function in discovery, when things are as yet too uncertain to be precisely articulated. This was discussed by Janet Martin Soskice and Nick Spencer in conversation about 'dead metaphors:' those which were originally deployed metaphorically but have now entered the lexicon as formal descriptions, like the current and flow of electricity; that a wire is live; or that an organism has cells. Even when talking about something as straightforward as wine we talk about it being crisp, dry, firm, flat, heavy, sharp, supple, tart, and velvety, as though these were accurate descriptions in fact. Spencer notes that metaphors like the 'selfish gene' function as a way of creating a conceptual universe for something where no detailed vocabulary is yet available. Soskice draws the parallel with scientific models which may be physical or mathematical, but may also be models of language (metaphors), like describing light as waves, or describing electricity as fluid, which then generates a language that can be used to test the theory or concept: What if it was really like a fluid? Would it then flow? Would it then have a current?[5] It may therefore be that science is premature to condemn consciousness to the realm of sophistry and illusion, just because humans have not yet found a way to correctly articulate it.

The ability through metaphor to be oblique but meaningful is a particularly human gift. The academic Iain McGilchrist would explain this with reference to his thesis of the divided brain.[6] He argues that the brain's left hemisphere is designed to facilitate the kind of narrow attention an animal or a person would need to focus on the task in hand, while their right hemisphere keeps watch for anything that might interrupt them, and to make broad connections with the outside world. So the right hemisphere gives sustained, broad, open vigilance, and alertness, where the left hemisphere gives narrow, sharply focused attention to detail. With our left hemisphere we grasp things in our hands and make tools; in language our left hemisphere similarly 'grasps' things by pinning them down and being precise. To do this we need a simplified version of reality, a sort of mental summary, so that we are not distracted by complexity. Meanwhile the right hemisphere is alert for exceptions and things that might be different from what we expect. It sees things in context and apprehends meaning and metaphor, body language, and the emotions.

> Let me make it very clear: for imagination you need both hemispheres. Let me make it clear: for reason you need both hemispheres. So if I had to sum it up I'd say the world of the left hemisphere, dependent on denotative language and abstraction, yields clarity and power to manipulate things that are known, fixed, static, isolated, decontextualised, explicit, general in nature but ultimately lifeless. The right hemisphere by contrast yields a world of individual, changing, evolving, interconnected, implicit, incarnate living beings within the context of the lived world, but in the nature of things never fully graspable, never perfectly known and to this world it exists in a certain relationship.[7]

Commenting on his book's title, *The Master and His Emissary*, he quotes Einstein saying that the intuitive mind is a sacred gift and the rational mind a faithful servant, but 'we have created a society that honours the servant but has forgotten the gift.'[8]

This thesis makes short work of a pressing problem in consciousness. The Binding Problem is the name given to trying to understand what goes on when our consciousness is able to solve the 'segregation problem' by being able to separate perceptions like colour and size into their constituent objects in a complex environment (like walking around a room and tuning into different conversations), while also being able to solve the 'combination problem' by being able to combine objects and features into a single experience (like seeing 'Mum'). Iain McGilchrist would simply explain this as the left and right brain hemispheres differentially kicking in.

That said, it should already be obvious that it is far easier for AI to copy the workings of the left hemisphere than to decipher the right; indeed it already has. In Hobbes' terminology, it is the left brain that does the computing, and this is largely what AI has sought to replicate. McGilchrist adds further complexity to the argument that brains achieve consciousness once they are complex enough, by arguing that *self-consciousness* is actually the left brain scrutinising the right brain.[9] So for those who subscribe to the view that consciousness is caused by the brain, the interplay between the hemispheres might well be a good place to look for answers.

McGilchrist writes his books because he is furious about the West's partiality for the left hemisphere. He argues that this deforms how we now live, so must be rebalanced to honour the right hemisphere if society is to return to health. He argues that our addiction to systematising everything with our left brain has crowded out the role the right brain has to play in attending to meaning and purpose, which is why so many people are suffering from poor metal health. In the context of a discussion on AI, this left hemisphere bias is also behind the over-weaning control of empiricism over the debate, and the McGilchrist thesis is yet another reminder that this suggests we may be missing something important. Incidentally, one of the disciplines he regards as useful for entertaining uncertainty and possibility and keeping the right brain supple is the soul's own discipline of theology: 'here faith can touch and handle things unseen.'[10] Like the use of metaphor, the leap of faith that religion requires allows concepts to be grasped and tested, which might otherwise feel impossible to entertain. And the sheer complexity of concepts like the Trinity or Jesus being wholly God and wholly man require extreme mental agility.

CONSCIOUSNESS

The field of study on consciousness has ebbed and flowed over the years. Usually characterised in philosophy as the 'mind-body problem,' it has been rather quiet of late, since the confident claims of the neuroscientists that they can explain everything through magnetic resonance imaging (MRI) scans. It also seems to have fallen out of intellectual fashion because of traditional links to metaphysics and the religious idea of the soul. Philosophers were also cowed by Gilbert Ryle's 'Ghost in the Machine' condemnation of the entire intellectual effort as a category mistake. His argument that mind and body are simply not comparable effectively killed the whole conversation stone dead, because no-one has yet thought of a more universally acceptable way to discuss them.[11]

But one hardy campaigner in the field of consciousness remains the philosopher Thomas Nagel. In 1974 he wrote a ground-breaking paper published in *The Philosophical Review* called 'What Is It Like to Be a Bat?'.[12] In it, he argued that the fact that an organism has conscious experience at all means that there is something it is like to *be* that organism. This established the axiom that for an organism to have conscious mental states it has to have a subjective sense of 'what it's like' to be that organism, whether bat or human. It is this subjective character of the experience of consciousness which militates against its objective description: we cannot know what it is like to be a bat unless we are one, because that phenomenological experience is not available to us. You can dissect my brain and tell me everything there is to know about it, apart from what it feels like to be me. And the fact that as a human I cannot explain what it is like to be a bat demonstrates that there are facts that exist (bat-ness) which are not expressible in a human language. But this lack of words does not airbrush out the reality of bat-ness. Science is therefore the wrong tool for understanding consciousness, as it can only deal in objectivities: 'conscious subjects and their mental lives are inescapable components of reality not describable by the physical sciences.'[13]

He argues that the principles underlying the emergence of life may be teleological, rather than materialist or mechanistic, that is, they are not so much about what we already are and how we operate, as about why we are here or what we may become. As he concludes, the universe seems to be 'prone to generate life and mind' and while it is not yet proving susceptible to a final explanation beyond the religious does not mean that it never will be.[14] That means consciousness as a human phenomenon in our evolutionary life-cycle is salient because it is bound up in this teleology, and must therefore be purposeful. As a *systematic feature* of the natural world, just because we struggle to define or explain it does not mean that 'the lacing of organic life with a tincture of qualia'[15] is not manifest or pivotal. And given its clear if mysterious importance, any account of evolution that ignores it will be deficient.

It is this argument from evolution that consciousness must be purposeful that points up a key difference between humans and manufactured entities. We can step into the river and collect a sample to copy the water we find there, but it is not the river we are copying unless we understand its beginning and its end. Copying a human now, using only those tools available to us, might be better in terms of quality than copying an older evolutionary model, but it is unlikely to take into account future improvements either in evolution or in our understanding of our species. So a myopic focus on replicating just what we can readily explain, from a design point of view, is already theoretically suboptimal.

QUALIA

As in the quote above from Nagel, one of the ways that philosophers have developed to talk about consciousness is through the use of the notion of 'qualia.' In the field of philosophy of mind, 'qualia' are defined as individual instances of subjective, conscious experience, like experiencing the colour red. The philosopher Daniel Dennett summarises qualia as properties of a subject's mental states that are: (1) ineffable – you can only apprehend them by direct experience; (2) intrinsic – you feel them independently; (3) private – they are only ever truly yours, even if others appear to have similar experiences; and (4) directly or immediately apprehensible in consciousness – you know you're experiencing them when they happen.[16] Your current feeling of intrigue or puzzlement about this concept is a quale. It is argued by some that qualia are *irreducible*, that is, not susceptible to further simplification, while others reckon that disciplines such as quantum physics will further explain this phenomenon in due course.

One of the most famous discussions of qualia in the context of AI helps to explain the idea a bit more. In a 1980 paper that became an instant classic, the philosopher John Searle introduced a thought experiment called the Chinese Room (see Box 4.1).

This argument suggests that no matter how intelligently a computer behaves, there is a difference between achieving these results mindfully and achieving them mechanically. Searle himself draws a distinction between syntax and semantics, where the symbols are the syntax, but the kind of meaning-making that would be added to them by a person who knew the Chinese language would be semantics.[18] Google Translate is a familiar example of the Chinese Room; and the winning program in the International Conference on Document Analysis and Recognition in 2009 was a real life equivalent of this experiment, in which it won the

> **BOX 4.1   THE CHINESE ROOM**
>
> Imagine an English speaker who knows no Chinese locked in a room full of boxes of Chinese symbols, with a book of instructions for manipulating the symbols. Imagine that people outside the room send in other Chinese symbols which, unknown to the person in the room, are questions in Chinese. And imagine that, by following the instructions in the book, the person in the room is able to pass out Chinese symbols which are correct answers to the questions. The outputs would suggest that the person in the room knows Chinese, when in fact they do not understand a word of it.[17]

competition to recognise cursive handwriting in French, Arab, and Farsi, without any knowledge of the languages involved.

Another way of describing the difference between someone enacting 'Chinese' and someone knowing Chinese is to call it consciousness. In the Chinese Room, the person is not *knowing* about Chinese: they do not *understand* the language at all. So the philosopher Margaret Boden has argued that qualia like 'seeing bean-sprouts or understanding English' are properties of people, not of brains, so this thought experiment merely confirms that the animation of processes requires consciousness: we might puppet a corpse – or a machine – to act like a human but it would not be human without an ability to experience qualia.[19] In the 1997 film *Good Will Hunting*, this is elegantly summarised as the difference between knowing everything there is to know objectively about Michelangelo, versus knowing what it smells like in the Sistine Chapel.[20]

The qualia debate has therefore moved on to an investigation into how or in what way artificial intelligence might ever achieve consciousness. Some have argued that if consciousness is really just self-awareness, then as soon as a computer becomes aware of and reflective about its own processing, it could be deemed conscious. As Max Tegmark puts it, 'consciousness is the way information feels when being processed in certain complex ways.'[21] There is certainly a school of thought that consciousness only emerges when the brain gets complex enough. Some have drawn an analogy with solids turning into liquids, or with the generation of a magnetic field which relies on but is distinct from the magnet itself.[22] On this basis it is perfectly possible that AI could spontaneously become conscious when a threshold has been reached. The development of Hod Lipson's walking robot teaching itself to read faces would support this argument, albeit from an argument of need rather than neural complexity.[23] Informed by his perspective as an expert in robotics, he sees this as a very specific ability to build a virtual model of your own body in space. He thinks that once we achieve that kind of 'physical' self-simulation, we move on to do the same for our minds; and that AI will make the same evolutionary journey.[24]

It is not yet clear whether this constitutes a kind of 'consciousness' or at least a step towards it, or whether it matters. There are many examples of the body spontaneously developing capabilities. Not only is the brain plastic, but if the gut has a section removed it simply reprogrammes the rest of it to compensate. Bodies quietly heal themselves – or indeed kill themselves – and female bodies build babies without conscious instruction. But the spontaneous resourcefulness of Lipson's robot does challenge the argument that spontaneous consciousness is about reaching a threshold of neural complexity. AlphaGo is a more complex AI than Lipson's walker, but it could be argued that it didn't need to learn how to read faces in order to win, because that challenge is largely about mathematics. Lipson's walker, though, may be simpler in its neural design, but being able to process the feedback from observers was materially helpful to its goal, so as a deep learning neural network programmed with reinforcement learning it was essentially programmed to be resourceful in this way. Indeed, if Moravec's Paradox is right, we'd need consciousness more for the ancient human tasks like seeing and walking, when our brains were less complex than they are now, because consciousness provides richer feedback data for these kinds of activities. Babies, after all, are 100% qualia.[25]

That said, it is worth pausing to parse our disquiet with the Chinese Room trick before we go on. On the face of it, the scenario merely points out a category mistake – an AI that can generate meaningful Chinese will always be in a different category from a human person who actually *understands* Chinese and we should not confuse the two. But while the scenario is generally used to discuss the phenomena of consciousness and qualia, this does not really explain our disquietude about it. Do we feel fooled by the fact that the output has been produced without the benefit of the expected expertise, or are we just worried that the output is in some undiscernible way substandard because a Chinese speaker would have added more value? The first scruple is a moral one, and is not new. Ever since the Old Masters outsourced the draperies to their studios, and we learned that Bridget Riley and Damien Hirst did little more than give outlines to their students to complete, we have worried about authenticity. We always feel cheated if we pay for the expert but get the apprentice, which is why ghost-writers are seldom identified as the authors of the books they write for the great and the good. This issue of authorship and credit is why the legal field of intellectual property is so well-developed. This moral scruple about origin shades into the second one, a suspicion about quality. Would the painting have been better if the Old Master had done all of it, and would the quality of the Chinese have somehow been enhanced if the computation had been carried out by a Chinese language expert? We will return to the Chinese Room in the next chapter in the context of a discussion on epistemology, to see if this is really about quality, or rather about origination or provenance.

It may be that consciousness will finally prove to be somewhat material, and qualia reducible, and the most likely argument for this concerns quantum entanglement. Based on a 1935 paper authored by Albert Einstein, Boris Podolsky, and Nathan Rosen, quantum entanglement describes what Einstein later referred to as 'spooky action at a distance,' the theory that once a particle has interacted with another particle, they will 'remember' that entanglement, and this history will thereafter affect their behaviour. Particles from ancient stars still remember each other, even though they have been recycled into new matter. Championed at the time by Erwin Schrödinger, and more recently in the UK by Roger Penrose, some commentators argue that once we understand quantum physics, we will see that consciousness – and the collective unconscious – is nothing more than the 'spooky action' of entangled particles.[26]

This brief foray into the field of consciousness has established that consciousness, however elusive, is widely agreed to be a thing; its contested nature makes it undoubtedly a mysterious thing; its existence seems somehow to be important to our future survival as a species; and you can use the notion of qualia as way of differentiating between those who have it and those who do not. But this difficult fact remains: there is no current definition of consciousness that would exclude AI, should AI be able to argue compellingly for 'robot-ness.' This may just be a philosophical problem for now; but it will surely shade into a legal one if there is no improvement on definitions in philosophy, in law, and in rights. While many academics are hoping that one day we will be able to explain consciousness through further analysis of the brain, it is currently parked as the Hard Problem.[27] The 2021 Reith lecturer Stuart Russell went as far as to say that 'no-one I know is seriously working on that problem, so I have to just leave that problem for future generations because, like anybody else, I have no answer to those questions.'[28] But is there a more constructive way to address this problem?

NOTES

1 Stoppard, Tom (2015) *The Hard Problem,* London: Faber; first staged at the National, see https://en.wikipedia.org/wiki/The_Hard_Problem.

2 Foster, Charles (2021) *Being a Human,* London: Profile, p321f.

3 McGilchrist, Iain (2021) *The Matter With Things,* Vol II, London: Perspectiva, p1038.

4 As the famous 2nd Century Sceptic Sextus Empiricus put it, doubt properly acts as a laxative, washing itself away along with the dubious claims it tests, see Hallie, Philip (1985) 'Classical Scepticism—A Polemical Introduction,' in *Sextus Empiricus,* ed Phillip Hallie (Indianapolis: Hackett), p7. See also Wittgenstein's famous conclusion 'whereof we cannot speak thereof we must be silent' in Wittgenstein, Ludwig (2016) *Tractatus Logico-Philosophicus,* trans Ogden, CK, Asheville, NC: Chiron Academic Press, p90.

5 See The Reading Our Times podcast, 7 December 2021, on the Theos website at https://www.theosthinktank.co.uk/comment/2021/12/07/how-on-earth-should-we-talk-about-god and Soskice, JM (1985) *Metaphor and Religious Language,* Oxford: Clarendon Press.

6 See McGilchrist, Iain (2009) *The Master and His Emissary,* New Haven, CT: Yale University Press, and also the useful RSA Animate which summarises the book with graphics at https://www.thersa.org/video/animates/2011/10/rsa-animate---the-divided-brain.

7 See p3 in the transcript for his talk for RSA Animate on 17 November 2010 https://www.thersa.org/video/animates/2011/10/rsa-animate---the-divided-brain.

8 See the final lines of his talk for RSA Animate on 17 November 2010 at https://www.thersa.org/video/animates/2011/10/rsa-animate---the-divided-brain.

9 McGilchrist, Iain (2009) *The Master and His Emissary,* New Haven, CT: Yale University Press, p224.

10 From the anthem is 'Here, O my Lord' by Percy Whitlock (1903–1946), after a hymn by Horatius Bonar written in 1855.

11 Ryle, Gilbert (1990) *The Concept of Mind,* London: Penguin.

12 Nagel, T (1974) 'What is it like to be a bat?' *The Philosophical Review* 83:4, p435–450. It should be noted that as an atheist writing on consciousness, he seems to have more purchase in the academy than commentators on consciousness who are theologians, perhaps because his atheism suggests a degree of disinterestedness in metaphysics and any pressure to 'prove' the soul theologically.

13 Nagel, T (2012) *Mind and Cosmos,* Oxford, OUP, p41.

14 Ibid., p127.

15 Ibid., p44.

16 Dennett, Daniel C (1988) 'Quining qualia,' in Marcel, A & Bisiach, E, eds, *Consciousness in Modern Science,* Oxford: OUP, via http://cogprints.org/254/1/quinqual.htm.

17 See Searle, John R (1980) 'Minds, brains, and programs' *The Behavioral and Brain Sciences* 3, p417–457 and as summarised in Searle, John R (1999) 'The Chinese Room', in Wilson RA and Keil F, eds, *The MIT Encyclopaedia of the Cognitive Sciences,* Cambridge, MA: MIT Press.

18 Searle, John R (2004) *Mind*, Oxford: OUP, p63 and 70.

19 Boden MA (1988) *Computer Models of Mind*, Cambridge: CUP, p244.

20 See also the classic Mary's Room experiment, about a girl who is brought up in an environment designed to avoid her ever seeing the colour red. In the David Lodge riff on it in his novel *Thinks*, he has his character Helen assign her students the task of writing up the Mary's Room experiment in the style of a variety of modern novelists. In one of the stories, unbeknown to the scientist, the experiment has long-since failed, because he forgot to factor in Mary's frequent access to the colour red via her menstrual cycle. Lodge, David (2002) *Thinks*, London: Penguin, p164.

21 Tegmark, Max (2017) *Life 3.0*, London: Penguin, p301.

22 See for example the arguments for emergence of O'Connor and Hasker in Corcoran, K, ed (2001) *Soul, Body, and Survival*, Cornell: Cornell University Press, p50f and 116.

23 See the 2018 documentary *Do You Trust this Computer?* (http://doyoutrustthiscomputer.org/). Lipson would call this 'machine self-awareness' rather than consciousness and holds that 'self-awareness is probably an evolutionary advantage for humans, in many circumstances. And it evolved gradually' (private email, 4 February 2022).

24 See the July 2019 interview with Lipson in Quanta magazine at https://www.quantamagazine.org/hod-lipson-is-building-self-aware-robots-20190711/ and Chen, B, Kwiatkowski, R, Vondrick, C & Lipson, H (2022) 'Fully body visual self-modeling of robot morphologies,' *Science Robotics*, 7:68, eabn1944.

25 Just to throw another spanner in the works, some have argued that, because consciousness is only needed when the unconscious and the subconscious have failed, and both of these are more material than consciousness to the daily functioning of a human body, that they are the appropriate topic of study, rather than their inferior sibling. See for instance arguments in McGilchrist, Iain (2021) *The Matter With Things*, Vol II, London: Perspectiva, p1041f.

26 Foster, Charles (2021) *Being a Human*, London: Profile, p318–322.

27 For a good round-up of the state of the field on consciousness see https://www.theguardian.com/science/2015/jan/21/-sp-why-cant-worlds-greatest-minds-solve-mystery-consciousness. See also https://en.wikipedia.org/wiki/Hard_problem_of_consciousness.

28 As delivered on BBC Radio 4 live from Newcastle on 22 December 2021, see archived audio recording and transcript at https://www.bbc.co.uk/programmes/m0012q21. In his 2019 book he goes further, writing consciousness off as 'missing the point' because it is *competence* not consciousness that matters. I disagree. See Russell, Stuart (2020) *Human Compatible*, London: Penguin, p17.

CHAPTER 5

How Do We Know?

At the foundation of well-founded belief lies belief that is not founded.

Ludwig Wittgenstein

HOW WE KNOW THINGS

The Chinese Room is designed to raise questions about the limits of artificial intelligence but it also serves to ask the question about types and hierarchies of knowing or intelligence. In Searle's example, the semblance of knowing Chinese is inferior to actually knowing Chinese, even though they may appear to be the same. This suggests that it may be worth teasing out what we know about types of intelligence, and how susceptible each might be to being created artificially in a computer, in order to zero in on distinctively *human* intelligences.

What does the text in Box 5.1 mean? It means that I had crashed rather badly skiing and needed to have my knee rebuilt. Usually we are scathing about jargon, because it feels obfuscatory and not clarifying. Bad academics hide behind it,[1] but the MRI example explains why it can be the most precise way to avoid misunderstanding, in a field where cutting into the wrong part of the body might actually prove fatal.[2] In the field of knowledge, there is a lot of jargon, in order to be supremely careful with meaning. So please use the Glossary at the end of the book for this section.

To start with, *ontology* is the philosophical field concerning the nature of reality. *Epistemology* is the philosophical field concerning the study of knowledge, so ontology is *what* we know, and epistemology is *how* we know it. This is important in our discussion about artificial intelligence not

DOI: 10.1201/9781003366614-5

BOX 5.1 MRI 2006

The menisci are intact. There is a partial tear of the MCL. The ACL is thickened, with quite a vertical orientation, and the appearances are in keeping with at least a partial tear, and I suspect the tendon is completely torn. There is diffuse oedema within the proximal tibia, which is maximal in the postero-lateral corner, and this appearance would be in keeping with an impaction injury following ACL tear. The oedema that surrounds the MCL tracks proximally to involve the medial retinaculum. There is subcutaneous oedema adjacent to the patella. There is some oedema within the patellar articular cartilage, with a small full-thickness cleft within the articular cartilage of the lateral facet. The patella tendon is intact. CONCLUSION: Partial tear of the MCL, with involvement of the medial retinaculum. Thickened ACL, with evidence of an impaction injury in the postero-lateral corner of the tibial plateau and these findings would be strongly suggestive of a complete tear of the ACL. Intact menisci. Subcutaneous oedema anteriorly.

---

only because we are trying to understand the basic reality of persons and consciousness (their ontology), but we are trying to clarify the extent to which artificial intelligence can theoretically replicate our own. It is therefore easy to see that we could program a lot of ontology into a robot, like populating Wikipedia. The extraordinary generative pre-trained transformer (GPT) tools are a good example of this. The company OpenAI has programmed them to generate reliable content like news stories or fiction by hoovering up the internet. The public release of ChatGPT in November 2022 fuelled a frenzied discussion about plagiarism as both students and academics rushed to use it for course planning and essay writing.[3] Its outputs are so convincing they are raising complex questions about truth. For example, their GPT-3 tool can generate compelling Jewish theology, which being sourced from authoritative texts might be considered authoritative, in spite of its artificial collation.[4] It is a beautifully current example of the Chinese Room, and illustrates that our scruple is more focused on epistemology than ontology: the Chinese or the Midrash is correct, but we feel uncomfortable about its status because of how that knowledge was reached. Culturally in the West we have enshrined one version of this scruple in academic rules about plagiarism. In academia it is an automatic fail, and often a gross misconduct offence in employment, if you are found to have used another's material without appropriate acknowledgement. This raises the question of whether we would feel less uncomfortable if GPT-3's Midrash had 'shown its workings' by being fully referenced.

Back to epistemology, programming assumes a way of accessing knowledge that is based on data that currently exists, which is by definition already historical. In philosophical terms this favours a way of apprehending the world that is empiricist, material and sceptical: it is not real if it does not exist. This is the prevailing approach of science. But as we are discovering with bias in algorithms, it falls victim to the problem of garbage in/garbage out: you are only ever as good as your dataset.

The allure of data[5] means that in many fields a confusion has resulted between what is called positive and normative statements. Positive statements are statements of fact. In linguistical terms, they are expressed in the indicative mood. They simply are. They can be tested, and involve no value judgements. But normative statements shift this register up a notch, by opining on what *ought to be*. Linguistically deploying the imperative, they would translate the 'fact that x' into a 'rule that x,' so a statistic showing most senior jobs to be held by men might sidle into a belief that senior jobs should be held by men. In 2017, this particular error led Amazon to withdraw its recruitment AI, because in using a biased dataset its algorithms had converted the positive into the normative.[6] This sleight of hand is incredibly common and easy to miss, but it is a category mistake.[7]

In epistemology, empiricism is only half of the picture. Epistemology in general tends to be categorised by looking at the fundamental ways in which we know things, either in theory or in practice. Table 5.1 presents a simplified illustration of a typical range of epistemologies.

Today, fashion favours the right-hand column, which naturally privileges what would be called an empiricist mindset because of the reassuring and tangible proof that physical evidence provides. But ironically it is the rules and logic of the left-hand column that are the preoccupation of AI programmers. Both kinds of knowing can be taught to AI, because both pure reason and sense-experience are about logic and data. However, because sense-experience is enhanced by the phenomenological experience

TABLE 5.1   List of Epistemologies

Ways of Knowing That Can Be Worked Out in Your Head: True by Definition	Ways of Knowing That Require Outside Data: Proven Through Experience
A priori – H_2O in a liquid state will feel wet	A posteriori – I went out in the rain and I got wet
Analytic – the word rain connotes a wet thing	Synthetic – actual rain would prove this thesis
Necessary – rain will be wet, by definition, in all possible worlds	Contingent – we will not know if rain is wet until we have felt it, in all possible worlds

of qualia, it is still a proprietary property of being human, so currently needs to be programmed in second hand.

THINKING STYLES

As well as these traditional ways of knowing, it is worth considering what we have learned about how humans prefer to think. This is why the modern discipline of cognitive science now includes psychology as well as philosophy. How we think has been the preoccupation of generations of psychologists, and has turned into the science of personality. Commercialised by the management training industry, a vast array of psychometric tests emerged through the course of the last century. Because of scepticism about the range of models in use, all claiming distinctive authority, there was a move in the 1980s to apply factor analysis to the existing range of tests, in order to winnow out the reliable agreement between them. From the 1990s, the theory settled around the so-called 'big five' personality traits. Using scales, these are assessed as combinations of degrees of openness, conscientiousness, extraversion, agreeableness, and neuroticism.[8]

The Big Five are used in many contexts, and have recently become popular in big data and AI as a quick route towards instant segmentation and profiling, being the thinking behind the highly controversial use of targeted advertising in recent US and UK elections. One of its leading lights is Michal Kosinski, now a professor at Stanford Graduate School of Business. In one study, his team applied a language-based assessment of the Big Five to 6,064,267 US Twitter accounts, mapping the data to 2,041 counties and triangulating with other political, economic, social, and health data available through surveys and government agencies. They found that Openness was higher on the coasts, Conscientiousness was uniformly spread, Extraversion was higher in southern states, and Agreeableness was higher in western states. Conscientiousness also correlated with increased life satisfaction. Notably, there was a higher Republican vote in less Agreeable counties.[9] This data harvesting, particularly using Facebook profiles, was the methodology used by Cambridge Analytica (see Steven Levy's book *Facebook: The Inside Story*) and created a global scandal about the unauthorised use of social media data for political manipulation.[10]

Regardless of this controversy, the theory underlying the Big Five would particularly implicate Openness and Agreeableness in thinking. Neuroticism might assume an audience, Conscientiousness might affect diligence, and Extraversion might attract company and speech, but it is preference on Openness and Agreeableness that guides preference on data and decision-making. The Openness scale is about preferred data, and the Agreeableness scale is about preferred decision-making: the former correlates to the more familiar labels from Jungian psychology of Intuition/Sensing, and the latter to Feeling/Thinking.[11]

The Openness domain is comprised of six facets or dimensions: openness to active imagination (fantasy), aesthetic sensitivity, attentiveness to inner feelings, preference for variety (adventurousness), intellectual curiosity, and challenging authority (psychological liberalism). Those who are more open will tend to be interested in patterns, possibility, and in attending to their so-called 'sixth sense.' Those who are less open will tend to shy away from these and take refuge in the concrete, the known, the tried and tested, and that which can be materially sensed. Because this trait is about the data you trust, the theory suggests that those who are less open feel at home with epistemologies that privilege facts and data, while those who are more open are constantly challenging these datasets.

The six facets that comprise Agreeableness are: trust, straightforwardness, altruism, compliance, modesty, and tender-mindedness. These are driven by a sense of what decision would be most suitable for or acceptable to others, because those who are more agreeable tend to be more empathetic; those who are less agreeable tend to be more selfish and would prefer more objectivity in decision-making. Because this trait is about decision-making, it suggests that those who are less agreeable will feel an affinity with the more objective 'scientific' method, whereas those who are more agreeable would worry about whether the subjective experience and feelings of ordinary people were being taken into account. The reality of this latter preference is probably why, particularly in the social sciences, there has been such an explosion in recent research methodologies that try to take phenomenology seriously, by converting it through scale into 'objective' data.

Whether or not you treat personality data as science or market research, the statistics are informative. In a general population, using the larger datasets available through the more established Myers Briggs psychometric tool (MBTI), there is a fairly even split in decision-making styles between those who are more or less agreeable, with a slight bias towards agreeableness in females, but the population data for the split between more or less open suggests that in a typical population around a quarter will prefer openness, and three quarters less openness in the type of information they trust, that is, a strong preference for scientific data.[12] Given that this is a general trend, and that people tend towards occupations that suit them, it is even more likely that those working in AI epitomise this bias, so it should not be surprising that there is such an overwhelming preference for empiricism.

In the same way that a particular philosophy may tell us more about how that philosopher thinks about thinking than about thinking itself, it is likely that AI programs similarly showcase how their programmers think about thinking. There is insufficient data to make generalisations about philosophers and type, or about those working in AI, but problems with algorithms have taught us to be alive to bias, and there may well be bias here. For instance, it is likely that those who object to the reductionism involved in materialist AI simply do not favour that prioritisation of data, because they feel it neglects something important that feels like relevant data to them.

This means we must tread carefully. It suggests that there is a strong bias in the established approach to AI, because of a strong epistemological preference in its community. As we have seen in the thinking of Iain McGilchrist, in the West this leaning would in any case be magnified by a cultural bias towards left-brain solutions which again favour particular concrete formulations of both problems and solutions.[13] This strong likelihood of bias is certainly a red flag for risk, and this blind spot about the relevance of other types of knowledge may well have already severely limited our design of AI.[14]

For our purposes, the Big Five personality traits are also interesting because of what brain imaging showed about them. As had been hypothesised, MRI scans showed that:

> Extraversion covaried with volume of medial orbitofrontal cortex, a brain region involved in processing reward information. Neuroticism covaried with volume of brain regions associated with threat, punishment, and negative affect. Agreeableness covaried with volume in regions that process information about the intentions and mental states of other individuals. Conscientiousness covaried with volume in lateral prefrontal cortex, a region involved in planning and the voluntary control of behavior.[15]

The dog that was not barking was any activity to show a biological response concerning Openness, the trait that is most concerned with intelligence-gathering, and particularly with regard to encouraging imagination, aesthetics, feelings, variety, curiosity, and the challenge of authority. This is presumably because while the performance or application of intelligence would be visible through brain activity, the property of 'being open' is an orientation not a thinking activity per se. But as we know, just because something is not 'there' on an MRI scan, does not mean that it does not exist, and is not important. The scientists recently re-learned that through what has to be the supreme scientific irony of recent times, the Higgs boson. Like Macavity, it's not there. It can only be proved by its absence, an infinitesimally small 'decay signature' that suggests that it might once have been. This proof, in absentia, is likely to be one of the most exciting scientific events of our age, so we underestimate the gaps between the data at our peril.

TYPES OF INTELLIGENCE

The alchemical step missed in the Chinese Room experiment was the moment of transformation when information was turned into outputs: the quandary was whether it mattered that this was achieved without the fairy dust of wisdom or knowledge. Is it material that the person in the room had no *understanding*? Does this make an output intrinsically faulty? If the 'computer' in the room was able in some non-human way to 'understand' would this change things? Conversely, what do we lose when it does not? As we have seen, the reduction of thinking to mere computation was championed by the philosopher Thomas Hobbes and as such represents the intellectual roots of AI.[16] It represents the thinning out of our understanding of thought thereafter, so before we conclude the discussion on knowing, it is helpful to develop the conversation on types of thinking into an examination of the ways in which types of knowing were historically understood beforehand.

Going back to basics, in Book 6 of his Nicomachean Ethics, Aristotle sets out the three foundational intellectual virtues: *episteme, techne*, and *phronesis*.[17] The first one gives us the English word epistemology, but in this context specifically refers to science; techne means art and craft; and phronesis means practical wisdom. Episteme is a person's intelligence about analytical and scientific knowledge, their ability to reason based on analysis and facts. It includes the epistemological categories in Table 5.1, and insofar as it is about assessing information and deriving conclusions, it is readily programmable into AI. Techne is about applying intelligence to making things, either through materials like wood or clay, or through media like song and dance. These craft skills are also programmable, in the way that professionals have always taught apprentices, or written instructional manuals. In both cases, there may be something additionally valuable in terms of feedback loops provided by time, experience, and qualia, but the volumes of data available would round out anomalies through training the AI on all known instances of similar activities.

Phronesis is rather less straightforward, being simultaneously better and worse done by humans, because phronesis is about value judgements and moral choice. Bent Flyvbjerg argues that Aristotle regarded it as the most important of the three intellectual virtues, because phronesis is where the instrumental rationality of the first two is balanced by value-rationality: it is where 'judgements and decisions are made in the manner of a virtuoso social and political actor,' and is of paramount importance 'because such balancing is crucial to the sustained happiness of the citizens in any society.'[18] Because it is the 'moral' virtue, it is best done by humans because of the complexity of their thinking, but it is also worse done by humans because of their tendency towards bias and error.

The Chinese Room can now be seen to be an experiment in examining what really constitutes the totality of 'knowing.' Setting aside the subjective quale of 'knowing' and focusing instead on what 'knowing' involves, we could argue that manipulating symbols based on rules and logic deploys both episteme and a degree of techne, but the lack of knowledge of Chinese limits the extent to which phronesis could be engaged.

In contrast to Aristotle, a further conceptual model also helps to zoom in on these distinctions. In a theoretical model of human intelligence posed by the psychologist Raymond Cattell in the 1960s, he drew a distinction between what he called crystallised intelligence and fluid intelligence.[19] Crystallised intelligence is like the internet. It is your personal database of facts and learning, which you google from time to time in order to find out what you know and make decisions. Fluid intelligence on the other hand is the ability to solve new problems, particularly when the existing data set is insufficient or there is a need to abstract from the known into novelty and invention. Like all models Cattell's theory is not a facsimile that would withstand prolonged neurobiological attention, but in this context it serves to conceptualise the Chinese Room as an exercise in the deployment of crystallised intelligence alone. There is nothing in play that does not exist and is not manifest, so there is no need for abstract creativity, just diligent rule-following. It is true that even a person who knew Chinese might also just be deploying their crystallised intelligence in this example too, in line with Hobbes' view of reason as reckoning. But our feeling of being short-changed might be because access to the fluid intelligence of a person who knew Chinese would act ask as a risk mitigation or a quality guarantee, to make assurance double sure: if the rules ran out, a person would be better equipped to improvise, than would be a tightly programmed machine. Indeed, this is precisely why there have been innovations in deep learning and Bayesian AI, to try to simulate this kind of abstract problem-solving.

Just to press this a little further and to be incredibly precise: by definition AI can deal with established ontology. It can deal with epistemologies that are about what is. It can use what is to generate projections about what might be, whether by pressing the positive into the normative or by calculating the mathematical odds on likely scenarios. It can deliver episteme, and techne based on precedent. It can also deliver phronesis based on rules and precedent, say by applying utilitarian calculus (as is currently the practice, e.g., with autonomous cars). What it cannot do (yet) is use qualia or use fluid intelligence to invent or create or abstract novelty, except where that novelty is derived from what currently exists. It can access data concerning the historical qualia of infinite human test subjects for as long as the species endures, but it cannot yet experience them. It is a theoretical possibility that sufficient data on human qualia will one day be available, such that AI would have synthetic access to it and not need conscious humans to supplement their own knowing. It also then follows that this may be sufficient for AI to make a case based on its own 'robot-ness' for a version of consciousness, under the current definitions in use.

Is that really it? Is that all we have got left, a shaky primacy based on qualia and a potential capacity for step-change innovation? Historically the argument about our distinctiveness as humans has been not just about our minds, but also about our souls, and to that topic we now turn.

NOTES

1 Because jargon is used to signal group membership, as well as to efficiently communicate, it also has a status compensation function, see Brown, ZC, Anicich, EM & Galinsky, AD (2020) 'Compensatory conspicuous communication: low status increases jargon use,' *Organizational Behavior and Human Decision Processes* 161, p274–290.

2 My favourite example from AI is this sentence: 'In 2007, Backpropagation was applied for the first time to neocognitron-inspired cresceptron-like (or hierarchical model & X-like) max-pooling convolutional neural networks

with alternating convolutional and max-pooling layers.' In section 5.16 of Schmidhuber, Jürgen (2015) 'Deep learning in neural networks: an overview,' *Neural Networks*, 61, p85–117.

3 See https://openai.com/blog/chatgpt/.

4 See https://forward.com/culture/469440/computers-can-write-torah-now-should-we-be-excited-or-terrified/.

5 We find data is so mesmerising that there is now a phenomenon of 'algorithm appreciation' whereby people trust the decisions of a computer more than they trust human decisions, see for example the research findings in Logg, JM, Minson, JA & Moore DA (2019) 'Algorithm appreciation: people prefer algorithmic to human judgment,' *Organizational Behavior and Human Decision Processes* 151, p90–103.

6 See https://www.reuters.com/article/us-amazon-com-jobs-automation-insight/amazon-scraps-secret-ai-recruiting-tool-that-showed-bias-against-women-idUSKCN1MK08G.

7 See the excellent discussion of David Hume's original formulation of the is/ought problem (Hume's Guillotine) in Gunkel, David J (2018) *Robot Rights*, Cambridge MA: MIT Press, p2f.

8 See summary of Big 5 tests in Gosling, SD, Rentfrow, PJ and Swann, WB Jr (2005) 'A very brief measure of the Big-Five personality domains,' *Journal of Research in Personality* 37:6, p504–528.

9 Giorgi, S, Le Nguyen, K, Eichstaedt, JC, Kern, ML, Yaden, DB, Kosinski, M, Seligman, MEP, Ungar, LH, Schwartz, HA, & Park, G (2021) 'Regional personality assessment through social media language,' *Journal of Personality* – online pre-publication at https://onlinelibrary.wiley.com/doi/10.1111/jopy.12674.

10 See also the June 2018 story in Wired magazine at https://www.wired.com/story/the-man-who-saw-the-dangers-of-cambridge-analytica/.

11 Furnham A, Mouttafi J, Crump J (2003) 'The relationship between the revised NEO-personality inventory and the Myers-Briggs type indicator,' *Social Behavior and Personality*, 31:6, p577–584.

12 Myers, IB, McCaulley, MH, Quenk, NL and Hammer, AL (1998) *MBTI Manual* 3rd Edition, Palo Alto, CA: CPP, p157f. See also Carr, M, Curd, J & Dent, F (2005) *MBTI Research into Distribution of Type*, Berkhamsted: Ashridge Business School.

13 McGilchrist, Iain (2021) *The Matter With Things*, Vol II, London: Perspectiva, p1111.

14 It cannot bode well that most AI is in the hands either of US corporations or the Chinese government, and the lack of transparency or regulation in this sphere means we cannot make an accurate estimate about bias in any case. More global involvement, and the scrutiny of it by more diverse global thinking, is likely to make our AI less limited.

15 DeYoung, CG, Hirsh, JB, Shane, MS, Papademetris, X, Rajeevan, N & Gray, JR (2010) 'Testing predictions from personality neuroscience: Brain structure and the Big Five,' *Psychological Science* 21:6, p820–828.

16 Williams, Stephen N 'Behind artificial intelligence,' in Wyatt, John & Williams, Stephen N, eds (2021) *The Robot Will See You Now*, London: SPCK, p46.

17 Thomson, JAK (1965) *The Ethics of Aristotle*, London: Penguin, pp171ff.

18 Flyvbjerg, Bent (2002) *Making Social Science Matter*, Cambridge: CUP, p2–4.

19 Cattell, RB (1963). 'Theory of fluid and crystallized intelligence: a critical experiment,' *Journal of Educational Psychology* 54:1, p1–22.

CHAPTER 6

The Soul

The hand of the Lord came upon me, and he brought me out by the spirit of the Lord and set me down in the middle of a valley; it was full of bones. He led me all around them; there were very many lying in the valley, and they were very dry.

He said to me, 'Mortal, can these bones live?' I answered, 'O Lord God, you know.'

Then he said to me, 'Prophesy to these bones, and say to them: O dry bones, hear the word of the Lord. Thus says the Lord God to these bones: I will cause breath to enter you, and you shall live. I will lay sinews on you, and will cause flesh to come upon you, and cover you with skin, and put breath in you, and you shall live; and you shall know that I am the Lord.'

So I prophesied as I had been commanded; and as I prophesied, suddenly there was a noise, a rattling, and the bones came together, bone to its bone. I looked, and there were sinews on them, and flesh had come upon them, and skin had covered them; but there was no breath in them.

Then he said to me, 'Prophesy to the breath, prophesy, mortal, and say to the breath: Thus says the Lord God: Come from the four winds, O breath, and breathe upon these slain, that they may live.'

DOI: 10.1201/9781003366614-6

> I prophesied as he commanded me, and the breath came into them, and they lived, and stood on their feet, a vast multitude.
>
> *Ezekiel 37:1–10*

HISTORY OF THE SOUL

Before we leave the topic of mind and consciousness, we need to examine the concept of the soul, which has so often in history been conflated with consciousness as the defining property of being human. This is because questions of mind depend on the answers you have already reached about the nature of your reality. If you have no reason to think that anything other than the Big Bang and evolution are in play, then your views on consciousness will be contingent on a materialist worldview. But for most of the history of the Philosophy of Mind, people believed that the world had been created by a God or gods, with particular purposes in mind, and with humans being the crowning manifestation of a sophisticated design. So it made 'folk' sense that our highest faculties must be the closest we can get to this intelligent designer, and might be their message to us or, in the case of the monotheistic religions, their hallmark in us. While it is fashionable to dismiss this 'folk' wisdom in the modern period, it has proved tenacious. In spite of numerous efforts to dislodge it, and through all the history and archaeology we know, faith is global in its reach and spread, and has not yet been categorically superseded as an explanatory narrative. This is because of the technical problem of trying to prove reality. A belief in reality, and therefore in any concept like a creator god, is by definition not provable, or falsifiable, because we cannot pop out of this world in order to check back on it. This means that the most honest position to hold is the ontological proof for God – or reality – that I call the Gruffalo Defence: just because we may have made something up, that doesn't mean it doesn't exist.

Looking at the western history of Philosophy of Mind to date,[1] the broad schools of thought about the soul might be summarised using the categories of materialism, dualism, and belief in god(s) (see Figure 6.1).

For most of the history of the Philosophy of Mind, metaphysics was naturally deployed to explain mind as soul, in a context where it was generally supposed that a deity or deities were responsible for our creation and had marked us out as special and precious through such a gift. As Goetz and Taliaferro put it in *A Brief History of the Soul*, 'the existence of the soul is more at home in a cosmos that is purposefully created by God'.[2] It was an

Materialism		God(s)	
Consciousness is a property of matter which emerges when a brain gets complex enough (**Emergentism**)	Matter is a property of consciousness, and emerges from it (**McGilchrist's Emergentism**)	Consciousness is the presence of immortal Soul (**Substance Dualism**)	**More Dualist**
	Consciousness exists; we do not fully understand it and cannot yet adequately explain it; so it should stay on our books until we can (**Agnosticism**)	Consciousness as an expression of soul is a God-given property of bodies (**Property Dualism**)	
Consciousness is an illusion; it is just an epiphenomenal side-effect of brain functioning (**Eliminativism**)	Everything is a mental event – our minds create our reality (**Idealism**)	The mental exists but is identical with the physical (**Physicalism**)	**More Monist**

FIGURE 6.1   Schools of thought on the soul.

intuitive way to explain so much that was not understood, and an immortal soul seemed to make sense out of death. One enterprising researcher famously tried to weigh the soul: in 1907, Duncan MacDougall reported that the difference post-mortem amounted to 21 g.[3]

In western thought, long before Christianity made the concept doctrine, the ancient Greek philosophers were carefully laying out parameters for a definition of soul. Generally they were what is now called 'dualist' because their lived experience taught them that the soul and the body were separate things, because animation visibly ceases with death when bodies are left behind to decay. What this means has given rise to vivid explanation in every civilisation known to us. For Plato (428–348 BC), the soul was the essential life or breath of a being. Because it was the soul that seemed to provide life, it must somehow *be* life, and must be immortal. It therefore came to be associated with things that are eternally true, which Plato calls the Forms. The Forms are universally perfect versions of things that exist imperfectly in our world. He famously explained this in his Allegory of the Cave, where humans sit and watch flickering shadows of the Forms, which exist in perfection as essential ideas elsewhere. This perhaps quaint and archaic idea has been picked up many times over the years, and in modernity it reappears as the notion that there is a perfect design somewhere, if only we could see it, and it is the animus behind all projects to perfect humanity, including AI.

There is more nuance in how Plato sees the soul, however, in that it is not all sublime. He thinks it has three parts. The base part, which plants also have, is **appetitive** and concerned with desire, pleasure and pain. The middle part of the soul, which animals also have, is the **spirited** part of the soul, which seems to act as a sort of charioteer or henchman, sorting out the appetitive part on behalf of the highest part of the soul, when they are out of kilter. This highest part of the soul, the part in communion with the Forms, is peculiarly human and is the rational or **intellectual** part of the soul. His disaggregation of the soul takes into account the full range of what we would now call consciousness, even if later accounts were prone to ascribe our 'animal' nature to our bodies rather than to our minds or souls.[4]

Plato's student Aristotle (384–322 BC) devoted a whole treatise to the soul. Written around 350 BC, it sets out all the entities that he believes have souls. As for Plato, Aristotle believed plants and animals had souls, although humans were the only entities that had a rational soul, or 'mind', which is both immaterial and eternal. This argument became known as the theory of hylomorphism, which holds that every being is comprised of matter and form. While he disagreed with Plato about the universality of Forms, he argued that in an individual our soul is to our body as form is to matter, and is that which animates our physical bodies. In his thinking, our soul is proprietary to us, not a manifestation of something universally generic.[5] Because matter is identical with potentiality and form with actuality, the soul is 'the first actuality of the body'[6] by which he means that its presence transforms a physical body from being *potentially* living to being *actually* alive. Without it, the body or entity is 'inanimate' and not a living thing (e.g., a robot). He further notes that when we see, we perceive that we see, and when we hear, we perceive that we hear. Whether or not we see and hear correctly does not alter this fact of perception.[7] This particular observation has proved a stumbling block for those (called Eliminativists) who would like to airbrush out qualia entirely: they still need to explain this phenomenon scientifically, given how stubbornly and universally observable it is.

Later traditions took up these themes of dualism and animation, layering in meaning about motivation and purpose in a more explicitly religious context.[8] Disastrously, possession of a soul was also weaponised to deny women and black people human rights.[9] In the medieval period, the concept of the soul acquired some very strong Christian branding, courtesy of St Augustine (354–430) and Thomas Aquinas (1225–1274). Although some have argued about the appropriation of the inheritance of Plato and Aristotle, in fact the Jewish and Christian scriptures which pre-date that tradition had always assumed the existence of soul. Both Augustine and Aquinas were concerned with establishing the Christian character of the human soul. As dualists, both were in the 'property' camp, which holds that the soul has no physical form, mainly because when it senses itself the soul does not sense that it has corporeality (Augustine). For Augustine too there was some preoccupation about where the soul came from (from Adam? From God? Recycled from other humans?), although Aquinas seems convinced that God populates every human with a soul, that improves in quality as the embryo grows, and somehow remains identifiably theirs even after they die, which makes their eventual reunion with our resurrected bodies practically possible.[10]

Bracketing the general intellectual foment of the Reformation, for our purposes Descartes (1596–1650) and *cogito ergo sum* are the next waypoint on the journey, with his famous thought experiment that has done more than anything else to establish the primacy of the mind. Although the materialists now argue that matter drives mind and not the other way round, it is this Cartesian crowning of the Greek tradition of the superiority of the intellect which may explain the modern choice of nomenclature: Artificial Intelligence rather than, for example, 'Artificial Humanity.'[11] He also rarifies the soul, by remitting Plato's lower parts of the soul to the body as mechanical functions, so that the soul becomes the vessel of the intellect alone. In a move that would gladden the hearts of today's neuroscientists, he also gives the soul a physical home in the pineal gland. And because he recovers the mechanical independence of the body, he departs from the idea that it is the soul that gives it life. He agrees that it is true that the soul departs on death, but because the body has died, not because the soul's departure is making it dead. It is this last development in thought that turns the future discourse from souls to minds and consciousness, and arguably away from the theologians and towards the philosophers. And that development in turn started to tether it to personhood as a property of some kind (rather than it being some kind of life-giving supernatural gift), so mind became a discussion about psychology and, more recently, about neuroscience.

That said, in recent years there has also been a surge in interest in workplace spirituality as a secular phenomenon, which had attracted a compelling body of academic work well before the emergence of mindfulness colouring books. This has required a revisitation and redefinition of soul for the new context, particularly in US academia where the field has deliberately distanced itself from religion and theology. The definitions in use in this literature tend to include purpose, values, meaning-making, being good or ethical, connectedness, transcendence, self-actualisation, and other-worldliness.[12] This discipline treats spirituality and soul as that realm or register of consciousness focused on higher purpose, not so much to conflate spirit or soul with consciousness, but to regard it as a particular and perhaps defining preoccupation of human consciousness.

In conclusion, most modern arguments on mind-brain now focus on debates about correlation and causality, rather than whether or not consciousness exists (except of course if you are an eliminativist like Daniel Dennett).[13] For instance, in view of developments in quantum physics that make matter seem immeasurably less concrete and substantial than was previously supposed, the argument that consciousness emerges from matter has been turned on its head by thinkers like Iain McGilchrist, who would argue that it is actually more reasonable to suppose that matter emerged from consciousness, in a deliberate attempt to self-limit through physical manifestation, which resonates with religious theories that would identify consciousness and the soul with God.[14]

It seems that the concept of the soul has not yet gone away or been somehow resolved or explained, it has just changed form in the debate. The underlying arguments remain, but the jargon about it changes, depending on the context in which it is being discussed. If one wants to talk about why we feel as though we have a mind that feels purposeful, if we have an ontology that embraces God, we talk about soul. If we are concerned that minds these days are rather too concerned with the profane or the mundane, we might talk about soul as a clarion call to return to the contemplation of higher things. If we are trying hard to be precise about the fronters of AI, we are more likely to talk about consciousness and qualia. In Wittgenstein's terms, these may just be different language games, the rules of which we give away by the register and jargon we deploy, but the questions they ask are the same questions that confronted the ancients: what is this unshakeable sense we have, that we have a personal and purposeful mind? Why do we have it, and where did it come from?

MAPPING SOUL TO CONSCIOUSNESS

In a famous lecture, the anthropologist Margaret Mead once brandished a human femur high above her head, pointing to the area on the thigh-bone where a fracture had healed over. She explained that this, more than a pot or a tool, was the first sign of civilisation: that a community had cared for one of its injured.[15] Because for much of the history of Philosophy of Mind, mind and soul have been conflated, the allergic reaction to religion in current intellectual circles serves as a useful discipline to drive precision. If mind in its most general sense maps to consciousness, how does soul map to them, if at all? In the disambiguation of consciousness, we looked at its philosophical definition as being an ability to experience qualia. In robotics, this idea of self-awareness has been further refined, because in robotics, as for humans, AI is embodied in a physical structure. Looking at how babies and toddlers learn, self-awareness in this context can be reduced – qua Lipson – to the very specific ability to draw up a mental map of your own spatiality in order to work out how to physically move.[16] Hod Lipson's robots learn to walk in the same way that toddlers do, through learning their bodies by trial and error. It is this capacity that permits our physical 'zero-shot' learning, whereby a human can size up an unfamiliar object and then move it, because we have already built up a spatial self-map and know how to tackle this kind of challenge. Lipson's approach helps to explain Emergentism rather better than AlphaGo can, because it is easier to see the evolutionary imperative of self-awareness when you consider how crucial consciousness would have been to the survival of a species gaining complexity in both brain and body. What the Princeton neuroscientist Michael Graziano calls 'semi-magical self-description' would have been vital to our day-to-day ability to find food and avoid predators, whereas learning how to be clever enough to win at Go is a luxury for a later phase.[17]

This certainly supports the argument of the Emergentists that on this logic AI will naturally evolve consciousness at the appropriate time, when the tasks it is given and the complexity of its wiring makes that an inevitability, in order for it to fulfil its function. AI would ultimately be able to experience qualia as data, and appreciate the colour red, because programmed into its logic would be the information it required to set this in context. Does this however somehow transform the computer in the Chinese Room into a person? Legally, perhaps: under Bostrom's rules, as soon as AI is both Sentient and Sapient it merits full moral personality and, in our current culture, full protection in law. But I think we would all want to argue that there is still something qualitatively different between AI learning to appreciate the colour red, and a human spontaneously doing so. In French this would be the difference between the verbs for knowing, savoir and connaître. Savoir is the kind of knowing that we can give AI; connaître, that familiarity with red, comes from somewhere else.[18]

But could this ever be a salient enough argument to hold weight, or is it just a wail of hurt from a species that once thought it was permanently special? There is an episode in the modern Dr Who franchise about a World War II monster, a child with a gasmask fused to his face who is turning the rest of London into gasmask-wearing monsters, all wandering around like zombies asking 'are you my mummy?' The problem is resolved when the Doctor realises that alien nanogenes, programmed for healing, had got the design of the first injured child they met wrong. Assuming that the gasmask was part of him, they 'healed' him with the gasmask attached. It is only when they 'learn' about his mother, by reading her DNA when she hugs her son, that they can reconfigure the infected humans as normal and the world is saved.

This story illustrates the difference between what is called source code and executable code. In programming, the first step is to write down what you want to do, then you compile this in machine code and operationalise it through executable code. The latter is the 'black box' that is handed over. You might copy the executable code, but if you have no access to the source code, you have to guess about the underlying logic and rules. This is essentially what we have been doing about fossils and geology and astronomy to come up with our theory of evolution and the Big Bang, and is the epistemology behind all of our inferred knowledge. It is also how we are explaining consciousness, yet I see behind consciousness a design that I would call the soul.

As we have seen from our analysis of schools of thought about the soul, there are a number of explanatory schemes for this state of affairs. If one believes in the concept at all, one is likely either to assume it is part of a design that has prospered through evolution, so must have a teleology linked to survival and success. Or one may glimpse a divine creator behind it, who has left behind their hallmark. Either way, it would be useful to understand as much as we can about it, and why we often act as though it is important.

This also immediately flags an issue with AI: if we are only copying across functionality that we see and perhaps poorly understand, are we designing in fused gas-masks? Could we do better? As Nick Bostrom argues, we are badly in need of fresh 'crucial considerations' and difficult original thinking to drive the next step-change in the development of AI.[19] Might trying to understand the soul take us to the next level? But the problem is, the soul is not a 'knowable item'[20] and if we stare at it for long enough, it does not look like a perfect Form: all we see is junk code.

NOTES

1 I am keenly aware that this summary is necessarily biased towards western scholarship, given the limitations of my own education and language skills. For an English-language introduction to the concept of the soul in non-western thought, given the lack of a one-volume global summary, it is worth reviewing the links in Wikipedia: https://en.wikipedia.org/wiki/Soul, or pursuing Robert Geraci on Hinduism, Tu Weiming on Confucianism, Jawanza Clark on indigenous black theologies, and those writing on the rich and diverse thinking of the indigenous peoples of North America and Australia. While global traditions vary widely, internationally the notion of the soul seems to find common ground as terminology for something that feels to humans somehow beyond the material and which is often viewed as having an eternal existence of some kind.

2 Goetz S & Taliaferro C (2011) *A Brief History of the Soul*, Chichester: Wiley-Blackwell, p209. Another excellent survey is to be found in Cottingham, John (2020) *In Search of the Soul*, Princeton, NJ: Princeton University Press.

3 MacDougall, Duncan (1907) 'Hypothesis concerning soul substance together with experimental evidence of the existence of such a substance,' *Journal of the American Society for Psychical Research* 1:5, p237–275.

4 See the useful summary in Goetz S & Taliaferro C (2011) *A Brief History of the Soul*, Chichester: Wiley-Blackwell, p15f. Many have commented on the similarities between this scheme and Freud's later idea in psychoanalysis of the id, the superego and the ego.

5 See Fine, G (1983) 'Plato and Aristotle on form and substance,' *Proceedings of the Cambridge Philological Society*, 29, p23–47.

6 See the opening argument in Book Two of 'On the Soul,' for example as translated by Hicks, RD (1907) *Aristotle's De Anima*, Cambridge: CUP, Section 412.

7 See the rather convoluted argument in Book Three of On the Soul, for example as translated by Hicks, RD (1907) *Aristotle's De Anima*, Cambridge: CUP, Section 425; or as summarised by Aristotle in Thomson JAK (1965) *Aristotle's Nichomachean Ethics*, London: Penguin, Book 9, Chapter 9, in his conversation about friends (p279).

8 There is even a theory based on passages in the Christian bible called trichotomism, which holds that human beings have bodies, souls *and* spirits, see Gooder, Paula (2016) *Body*, London: SPCK, p26 and 30.

9 See Hood, Robert E (1994) *Begrimed and Black*, Minneapolis, MN: Fortress Press, p138f.

10 The modern philosopher Eleonore Stump has a neat explanation for this, that souls are somehow tagged on the basis of their history, for ease of future identification once they have been absorbed back into the ether, see Stump, E (2003) *Aquinas*, New York: Routledge, p54.

11 See also the discussion of the western preference for mind over body as compared to the cultural influences in favour of robots in Japan, Geraci, RM (2006) 'Spiritual robots: religion and our scientific view of the natural world,' *Theology and Science* 4:3, p229–246.

12 Poole, E (2009) 'Organisational spirituality,' *Journal of Business Ethics* 84:4, p577–588.

13 See Dennett, Daniel C (1993) *Consciousness Explained*, London: Penguin.

14 McGilchrist, Iain (2021) *The Matter With Things*, Vol II, London: Perspectiva, pp1062ff. See for example the famous articulation at the start of the Christian Gospel of John: In the beginning was the Word, and the Word was with God, and the Word was God... and the Word became flesh and dwelt among us (RSV).

15 Cited in Brand, P & Yancey, P (2010) *Fearfully and Wonderfully Made*, Grand Rapids, MI: Zondervan, p82.

16 See this description of robot self-modelling: https://www.engineering. columbia.edu/news/hod-lipson-robot-self-awareness.

17 See Graziano, Michael (2018) *The Spaces Between Us: A Story of Neuroscience, Evolution, and Human Nature*, New York: OUP, as summarised in his 2016 article on Attention Schema Theory (AST) at https://www.theatlantic. com/science/archive/2016/06/how-consciousness-evolved/485558/.

18 There is a similar distinction in German (and no doubt many other languages) between wissen and kennen, where wissen is about knowing facts (like savoir), and kennen is about familiarity (like connaître).

19 See his plea in the conclusion of his book, Bostrom, Nick (2017) *Superintelligence*, Oxford: OUP, p317.

20 Spufford, Francis (2012) *Unapologetic*, London: Faber & Faber, p21.

CHAPTER 7

Junk Code

Nothing to see here?

What is greater than God and more evil than the devil? The poor have it, the rich need it; and if you eat it, you'll die. The answer is: Nothing. Nothing is greater than God, nothing is more evil than the devil; the poor have nothing and the rich need nothing. If you eat nothing, you'll die.

Nothing is an amazing idea. Without the invention of zero, computer programming would not exist. And nothing can add magic, if someone is on hand to add that vital nothing at the crucial moment.

There once was a Bedouin who had 3 sons and 17 camels. In his will, he left half of his 17 camels to his elder son, one-third to his second son, and one-ninth to his youngest son. When the father died, the children attempted to divide the camels according to their father's will, and struggled to divide 17 camels into one-half, one-third, and one-ninth. They went to consult a very wise old man, who said: 'Simple. I will lend you my camel. It will be the 18th, and you can get what your father wanted you to have.' Eureka! Half of 18 is nine, a third of 18 is six, and a ninth of 18 is two, making a total of 17. The sons divided up the camels, then the wise old man took his camel home.

Adding nothing can be important. 'It was nothing' we say every time we help someone.

So nothing is really quite something.

JUNK CODE?

In Ian McEwen's novel *Machines Like Me*, his robot protagonist Adam argues that fiction only works as a genre because it describes human

DOI: 10.1201/9781003366614-7

failure, and will be rendered obsolete as soon as 'the marriage of men and women to machines is complete.'[1] This rejection of fiction is an echo of the kind of revulsion that Spock the Vulcan feels on the Starship Enterprise whenever Captain Kirk gets emotional: non-humans, rationally built, with a horror of irrationality and error, very much see emotion as a failure of design or programming, even if it makes great TV. In just the latest treatment of this familiar SF theme, the 2021 film *Ron's Gone Wrong* is about a race to destroy a glitchy robot who has become too friendly with his owner. It is undoubtedly true that if robots behaved like humans they would have been turned off by now, or taken back to the shop for a refund.

In computer programming, junk code is redundant code that could be deleted or rewritten in shorter syntax without affecting the execution of the program. The code could be redundant because it was never executed (unreachable code), or because when executed it had no effect (dead code). Junk code is deliberately deployed by programmers to obfuscate and discourage copying, and by hackers to cast lures to avoid detection by automatic anti-cheat software. And it seems that we may have dismissed as junk code in our own programming something that is not redundant at all, which is in fact crucial to our core programming. Instead of being dismissed, this should be articulated, nurtured, and protected; but also mined for insight into how this mindset is limiting AI. Perhaps Junk Code is actually soul; and that it is not our consciousness that makes us special, but our souls. They are not perfect as would be implied by Plato's Forms: but are perfectly imperfect, and for good reason.

Our junk code shows up in several categories. The most famous is our very messy emotions, closely followed by our unshakeable ability to keep on making mistakes. We are also inclined to tell stories, are attuned to an uncanny Sixth Sense (which might of course be brain spasms of some kind), and we have an amazing capacity to cope with uncertainty. We also have a persistent sense of our own agency in the shape of free will, and a propensity to see meaning in the world around us.[2]

Emotions

In 2013, a burial was discovered in the Panga ya Saidi cave in Kenya. The grave was of a human child, estimated to have died just before they were three. The child was carefully buried wrapped in a cloth, with their knees tucked underneath their chin, and their head resting on a pillow. At 78,000 years old, this grave is the oldest one ever discovered. The archaeologists have christened the remains Mtoto, from the Swahili word for child.[3] The emotion behind this burial echoes down the millennia since this child died.

Down the centuries, another burial tugs at our heartstrings: the poet Philip Larkin's famous Arundel Tomb. Dating from the 1370s and situated in the north aisle of Chichester Cathedral, the recumbent figures of the Earl of Arundel and his second wife, Eleanor of Lancaster, lie side by side immortalised in stone. Dressed in his suit of armour, Sir Richard has one hand withdrawn from its gauntlet, reaching across to hold Eleanor's. The sight so moved Larkin that he wrote a poem about it, concluding with the famous line: 'what will survive of us is love.'[4]

In the centuries in between these deaths, other ancient finds bear witness to the emotions of our ancestors, both human and neanderthal, like the early cave paintings celebrating hunting and dancing, ancient fragments of toys and jewellery, enormous statues and artefacts of war, and our very earliest literature and drama. And ever since Charles Darwin's 1872 book on *The Expression of the Emotions in Man and Animals*, there have been repeated attempts within academic circles to both map the emotions and to explain their role in our evolution.

In 2015 Disney/Pixar released a film called *Inside Out* that used animation to portray the emotions in the head of an 11-year-old girl called Riley. Advised by the Emotion Psychologist Paul Ekman, the film featured Joy, Sadness, Fear, Anger, and Disgust, as versions of five of his universal basic emotions; Surprise and Contempt being the others. During his career he identified a list of 15 basic emotions (see Table 7.1).[5] These he would argue are universal, and do not vary by gender, race, or geography, but over which the local culture controls the volume button.

Ekman omits from his list those feelings he calls moods (which last longer than emotions), personality traits (like hostility), and 'emotional plots' which contain myriad emotions, like romantic or parental love/hate, grief, and jealousy.[6]

It is interesting to review his criteria for a universal basic emotion (see Box 7.1).[7]

There has been an explosion of interest in mapping human emotion because of the data this provides to AI. With humans who struggle with emotions, these kinds of lists have been used to train both recognition and response, much as we would with AI. The problem is that humans are brilliant at spotting both delay and pretence, because of criteria 3 and 9: we can instantly tell if something is learned and not automatic, and we can tell if it is genuinely unbidden or just hurriedly retrofitted. It will be

TABLE 7.1   Ekman's Basic Emotions

Basic Emotion

Amusement

Anger

Contempt

Contentment/Happiness/Joy

Disgust

Embarrassment

Excitement

Fear

Guilt

Pride in achievement

Relief

Sadness/Distress

Satisfaction

Sensory pleasure

Shame

BOX 7.1   EKMAN'S CRITERIA FOR A BASIC EMOTION

1. It must have distinctive universal signals (like the facial expression for surprise)
2. It must have distinct and characteristic physiological responses (e.g., a flinch)
3. It must be induced automatically (i.e., non-conscious or involuntary)
4. It must have distinct antecedents or triggers (e.g., rotten meat)
5. It must emerge distinctively in infancy
6. It must be present in other primates
7. It must be quick onset
8. It must be of brief duration
9. It must be an unbidden occurrence
10. It must be associated with distinctive thoughts, memories, and images
11. It must be a distinctive subjective experience.

interesting to see if the processing time of AI might ameliorate this problem for social robots in the future.

For humans, emotions seem to play a vital part not only in our experience but also in our survival. We know this because of the evolution of the brain. The most ancient parts of the limbic system are the amygdalae, two matching right and left almond-shapes buried deep in our temporal lobes. These play a primary role in not only our experience of emotion, but also in the formation of our memories. Their existence acts as a very physical neurobiological proof for Darwin's thesis about the crucial role of emotions in our evolution. This is because it is the amygdalae that are in charge of the brain's filing systems, and are the final arbiters on memory consolidation. So anything that occurs that is emotionally weighty is tagged as a particularly salient memory, to facilitate ease of retrieval under pressure should a similar challenge arise in the future. Even more so than the qualitative contribution emotions make to our lives, it is this system of the tagging of useful memories that plays such a crucial role in our future safety and happiness, by the maintenance of an emotional play-list designed to resource us when we are most in need.[8]

Mistakes

All humans are what Kathryn Schulz would call 'wrongitioners' because we make mistakes all the time.[9] That is largely why we are so keen to deploy AI as a tool in the first place. Some of our mistakes are because of our stupidity, forgetfulness, or lack of knowledge; and others are because our emotions lead us astray. They can be sins both of omission and of commission. As the Book of Common Prayer famously puts it, 'we have left undone those things which we ought to have done, and we have done those things which we ought not to have done.' Throughout history, human error has been both catastrophic and tragic, so it is unsurprising that we wish to design it away. But mistakes have also discovered x-rays and penicillin, invented the pacemaker, and cured erectile disfunction, so it might not be safe to program them out willy-nilly.

Trial and error are already important concepts in AI and are why Reinforcement Learning was developed. It is easy to see why babies and toddlers 'make mistakes' when they are trying to learn how to speak and how to move. But it is not long before they start making wilful mistakes rather than accidental errors. The literature on irrationality in human decision-making is well-established, with the recent bestsellers *Predictably Irrational*[10] and *Thinking Fast and Slow*[11] epitomising the genre. We know that we are prone to all kinds of thinking traps. But mistakes of this kind are not for me the essence of our junk code. Errors are after all the route to learning. All those failed experiments force the kind of adjustments that create breakthroughs and innovation, and this general bumbling around is what we trust will teach AI how to learn and how to be truly clever.

The junk code that I am interested in is moral error, or what Francis Spufford calls our 'active inclination to break stuff' which he has heroically dubbed the HPtFtU.[12] This is 'elusive to summarise but unmistakeable when seen: a certain self-pleasing smirk.'[13] It is that gleeful look in a toddler's eye when they bash their twin over the head with a toy. It is also our tendency to lie, usually for our own gain.[14] It is a human property that arrives early and stays late, and one that has lots of names. For instance, the theological literature on sin is legion in any religion you care to investigate.

In this context, the salient points are: moral error is a human phenomenon; religion is one of the structures that tries to cope with it ethically; and societies develop a rule of law in order to cope with it practically. So there is an important whiff of rule-breaking about this kind of mistake. It is not just mixing the petri dishes up; it is wilfully stealing another's lab results and passing them off as one's own. But it is the feeling that this kind of wrong-doing creates in us that is the crucial part: it is not so much that we make these kinds of mistakes, but that we tend to rue them afterwards. Indeed, those who cannot feel remorse are called psychopaths, and we regard them as lacking an essential human quality. In his *Theory of Moral Sentiments*, Adam Smith introduces the notion of the Impartial Observer, being a conscience that makes us try to behave. The sense of being watched is why commentators think that those of religious belief are more likely than atheists to obey the law, because in their philosophy God is always watching.[15] It is for this reason that the philosopher Soren Kierkegaard called remorse one of 'eternity's emissaries,' because its shadowy presence keeps us right.[16] This junk code is also therefore a superpower because of what it drives us to do. While rules shift by context and continent, this innate capacity for guilt does not leave us. This feeling of shame is what drives us to try to repair any damage we have done, and to resolve to do better in future. So it is vital societal glue, both for the regulation of communities, and for their reform.

As Anthony Bash has argued, feelings of remorse can only be metabolised through acts of repentance, so a well-developed ability to have an uncomfortable feeling like this, that cries out for resolution, is necessary to turn it from a 'noun' into a 'verb.' With it, remorse is virtuous. Without it, the emotion is not useful to humanity: it just festers and causes psychological harm.[17]

We want to design perfect AI. But would we want to design perfect beings? It is only this capacity to err and the conscience that tries to stop us that drives personal improvement. Arguably it also drives societal improvement, as we try to mend the wrongs we see around us. And while 'normal' error is crucial to general improvement, this kind of improvement in character is an investment in the health of our souls. This is one of the reasons that the theologian John Hick pounced on something interesting that the poet John Keats said about the world; in a letter dated 21 April 1819, John Keats wrote to his brother George to say that rather than writing off the world 'a vale of tears' he thought we should start calling it 'the vale of soul-making.' How else could souls be made; 'how but by the medium of a world like this? Do you not see how necessary a world of pains and troubles is to school an Intelligence and make it a soul? A place where the heart must feel and suffer in a thousand diverse ways.'[18] Hick took this notion of the vale of soul-making and made it a cornerstone of his theodicy, because being already a theist he was more interested in *why* we have a soul, rather than what it is or where it comes from.

Drawing on Irenaean theology from the early Hellenistic period of the Christian Church's life, he argued that a soul is not created in a finished state, it is still in the process of creation. Irenaeus was a Greek Bishop (c130–c202) who believed that while people were made in the *image* of God, they still needed to achieve his *likeness* through the exercise of their God-given agency and free will. This process of perfection is therefore taking place 'through a hazardous adventure in individual freedom.'[19] In this context, he was also talking about the kind of learning that comes from hard knocks and setbacks, as well as from the guilt of self-induced mistakes. For Hick, this explains the vicissitudes of life: our souls would have nothing to learn from, if everything went our way. Whether or not you like the idea of God testing us in the mighty amphitheatre of life, this key point about the soul's journey and development is otherwise neglected in the mind-brain literature. But given that the AI project is fundamentally about improvement, it is important to see this as one of the ways in which our junk code tries to promote improvement in us.[20]

Could we code character in? In a way we already do. As we have seen, in the human brain, salient emotional learning events are stored in the amygdalae for handy retrieval under pressure. So it becomes possible to acquire behavioural templates to make challenging situations easier to bear. So far so good – that is exactly how computer programming works too. But the difference is that humans need these templates to stop their emotional autopilot taking over in times of stress, which is not a problem that current AI will ever face. For humans, character is a coping strategy for adversity.

Storytelling

What was the first story you ever heard? Perhaps it was a fairy tale, or a children's book. Maybe it was a tale in a nursery rhyme, or a song; or something read out to you in a church or a temple.

By the time that Mtoto died 78,000 years ago, that child had probably already heard hundreds of stories round the fire, designed to teach them how to stay safe. Storytelling is one of our superpowers, and every culture that we know of has had a distinctive way of communicating their history and values through story. Until very recently in human history this was an oral tradition, so it was infinitely flexible. Amid the differences are clear themes about creation and good and evil, and even the stories that we have now written down, immediately get retold in different guises so that they keep their currency. It is probably not a very efficient way to communicate, but it seems to perfectly suit us.

In 1969, Christopher Booker set out to map this phenomenon. In the end it took him 34 years, to divide all known stories into seven basic plots (see Box 7.2). In doing so, he reached the remarkable conclusion that: 'there is no kind of story, however serious or however trivial, which does not ultimately spring from the same source: which is not shaped by the same archetypal rules and spun from the same universal language.'[21] For instance, folk-tale experts have collected well over 1000 versions of a 'Cinderella' story globally, so dispersed by geography and time that their similarity cannot be explained away by migration and trade routes.[22]

One by-product of his analysis is that it shows why the Lord of the Rings saga so endures, because it uniquely includes all seven of these basic plots. These seem in some way to be latent inside us, and when a storyteller finds a new and fresh way to tell back to us one of these classics, we immediately recognise it and respond. As Booker puts it, Jaws was just a re-telling of Beowulf, but an absolute classic of the Monster genre. And we adore the notion of evolution, because it makes us all stars in a Rags to Riches narrative. Conversely, when someone tells a story wrong we feel that they have 'lost the plot,' and when we read a book like that we feel dissatisfied, and somehow cheated or left hanging when we have finished it.

But not only do the plots inevitably recur, so does the standard cast of characters. Booker uses Jung's archetypes to explain this phenomenon. In psychology, Jung was to Freud probably what in philosophy Aristotle was to Plato. One of his particular contributions was the now-famous archetypes, standard characters identifiable from dreams and visions that Jung felt were manifested by humanity's collective unconscious, and were therefore fraught with meaning for guidance and advice, particularly in a clinical setting. Archetype theory is rather complex, but to give a flavour, the most famous archetypes are: Father, Mother, Child, Wise Old Man, Hero, Maiden, and Trickster.[23] So in a classic Quest, a Hero leaves a Mother and a Father (often having experienced trying Child circumstances) to rescue a Maiden; is thwarted by a Trickster but advised by a Wise Old Man; then returns with said Maiden to get married and become the next Father and Mother.

While it is distracting trying immediately to categorise all your favourite books and films into this scheme, one of his key messages is that he reckons that, at heart, all these stories are trying to tell us about consciousness and the risks of ego. All of the world's known mythology about the development of humanity contains stories about what happened to us when we became conscious and suddenly felt superior to the rest of creation. He would therefore agree with Ian McEwan that this is what literature is about – playing back to us all of our junk code so that we might learn from mistakes. Science Fiction casts this into the future, to warn us about the choices we might make next. In general, our response is to order more popcorn and be vastly entertained – it's just a story! We tell ourselves in relief.

As a race, humans inevitably act out our signature stories, both psychologically in our own lives and in society at large. We tap into them to justify expensive projects like Questing to the moon or Overcoming The Monster through invasion and warfare; and Rags to Riches means we disproportionately lionise the famous who used to be obscure. But what Booker's analysis shows is that our stories may actually be trying hard to tell us something important about who we really are. Emerging from our collective unconscious, they deploy the archetypes within the basic plots to teach us how to avoid alienation, and how to achieve reconciliation, not only within ourselves and our communities, but with the whole of creation.[24] Booker concludes that: 'if the evolution of human consciousness is really concerned with developing a clearer understanding of how we and the world work, perhaps the time has come when we should begin to appreciate what this astonishing faculty we each possess is really about.'[25] He points out, in stories that 'work' for a human audience, the story always resolves because of personal character, a capacity for ordered thinking, selflessness, and an ability to see the whole: love and reconciliation prevail and order is restored, whether it is Harry Potter or Shakespeare.[26]

Writers like Tolkien have argued that stories have a therapeutic use as well. In a lecture on 'fairy-stories' that he delivered in St Andrews on 8 March 1939, he argued that in introducing readers to a fantasy world that is properly internally consistent and rational, they can see better their own, and experience 'recovery' in the resolution that inevitably takes place in this parallel world. In this way a fairy story can provide 'consolation' through a happy ending. Tolkien coins the phrase 'eucatastrophe' to describe the 'piercing glimpse of joy' we get at 'the joyous turn' when our hero avoids peril and the story resolves.[27]

Booker was curious about not only our life-long obsession with stories, but also the human ability to conjure up images in our minds as they are being told to us: of course fiery dragons do not exist, but somehow we can 'see' them in our mind's eye. It is this capacity for stories to exercise the imagination which is the theme behind an appreciation of the coding that is our Sixth Sense.

Sixth Sense

Ever since Malcolm Gladwell wrote *Blink*[28] and then Daniel Kahneman wrote *Thinking, Fast and Slow*,[29] intuition has had a bad rap. These days everyone has decided that it is just lightning-quick processing, the fruits of years of learning and experience, which is fraught with bias to boot. The only reason we experience it as a Sixth Sense is because it happens so fast that we are not aware of our own processing. And insights from dreams and reveries? Just file retrieval from the subconscious.

But that sells this capacity too short. Intuition also includes visualisation and imagination. Even our empiricist friend David Hume would acknowledge the former, albeit in limited terms. His famous thought experiment about 'the missing shade of blue' argues that if someone was presented with a sequence of shades of blue ranging from dark to light, with one shade in the sequence missing, they would be able to visualise the missing shade.[30] Booker has already noted the phenomenon of us seeing characters from stories in our mind's eye, even if no illustrations are available, or if the characters are magical or invented. That is why there is always such a strong reaction when popular books are filmed or televised: Willy Wonka is not supposed to be creepy! That's not an orc! The hippogriff is all wrong! In the case of invented beasts, visualisation stretches into imagination, but imagination is also non-visual, and can be about the generation of new thoughts, ideas or theories. One example would be Hedy Lamarr discovering frequency hopping in the 1930s, when she imagined that transmitting radio signals along rapidly changing frequencies would help radio-guided weapons avoid detection and jamming.[31]

One puzzle in AI is how to decode seeing such that it could be accurately replicated. Apart from the fiendish complexity of the eye itself, our brains seem capable of extraordinary versatility in how we see: we 'zoom in' with our foveal vision, while also processing the generality of our environment with our peripheral vision. We make sense of glimpses or unclear images, and we are able to see both the rabbit and the duck in an optical illusion. Wittgenstein was increasingly intrigued by what he called this 'aspect perception,' being our ability to 'see that' and 'see as.'[32] We view a portrait and see the person. That is why we can both behold a set of shapes on a page and also 'read' them as language. Going back to the Chinese Room, the person being the computer manipulating the symbols is *seeing that* but not *seeing as*. In terms of our knowledge and understanding, Wittgenstein is interested in the difference between the before and after, but also in both the mental capacity and the felt sense at that moment of insight. When we transition from the one to the other, we are 'struck' by the dawning of an aspect; we light up when we finally 'see as,'[33] for instance when we decipher an optical illusion, or recognise something. 'Hence the flashing of an aspect on us seems half visual experience, half thought; the echo of a thought in sight.'[34] This is the 'aha' moment which is the best parallel for the quale of Archimedes shouting 'eureka!' and is similar to Tolkien's use of the term 'eucatastrophe' to describe that feeling too. This section of Wittgenstein's *Philosophical Investigations* is full of exuberant exclamation marks, and I would wager that a handy MRI brain scan from the moment he wrote it would look like fireworks.[35]

Of course the imagination can be chemically stimulated too. In 1797, the poet Samuel Taylor Coleridge awoke from an opium-induced dream with the whole of his poem Kubla Khan in his head. Having taken opium to ease the pain in his knees, he was interrupted while writing down his verses by the famously 'unfortunate man from Porlock.' By the time he left, the rest of the poem had left Coleridge's head too.[36] There is a long tradition of creatives using drugs to stimulate their thought process, which suggests there are biological ways to at least alter what we would call our

Sixth Sense, but it is too commonly observed in children for us to assume it is an unusual phenomenon that needs unusual stimulation.

But as Iain McGilchrist has argued, imagination is under attack as never before, given the dominance of the left-brain paradigm. It is extremely hard to see what is not there, and data can be mesmerising. Jargon like 'paradigm shifts' and 'thinking outside the box' are all appeals for us to rediscover and nurture this particularly human capacity. Another thinker who laments the death of the imagination is the theologian Paul Millbank. He argues that materialism has murdered the imagination, and that one of the biggest tragedies of modernity is 'our loss of faith in the visionary power of imagination to bring forth as yet unconceived possibilities.'[37] He notes that our children are allowed free rein in the imaginal realm, although we expect them to grow out of it, and artists and creatives are given social permission to explore the world of the imagination, but only in service of those in the real world who choose to fund them. The rest of us have to get real, and keep it real. His concern about this airbrushing out of an innate propensity is this: 'the fantasies which Realism dismisses as illusions may in fact be the whispers of a world waiting to be born. Imagination is a vehicle for the deepest moral intuitions of the human soul.'[38]

But we have already lost a lot of mental capacity through our use of tools, which does not bode well for the future. Before we could write things down, the bards could remember thousands of lines of poetry. The Odyssey alone stretches to over 20 hours of recitation. And if writing and literacy ruined our memories, inventions in music also changed our brains. Before the 14-year-old Mozart used musical notation to write it down for general consumption, you had to travel to the Sistine Chapel during Holy Week to hear Allegri's Miserere. Now the combination of notation and recording means we do not need to memorise music in order to hear it again. Even how we hear it has changed: in the West, before we trapped the scale to the equal temperament of the pianoforte we could both sing and hear the micro-tones, but even those with 'perfect pitch' can only pitch to a piano these days.

Even with a plastic brain that could be (re)trained with a capacity for imagination, it is still hard to see what is not there. That is why it is so important that we nurture this crucial element of our junk code, because it is trying to find us everything that isn't there. It can not only complete patchy datasets for us, but give us new insights and new data. It future-proofs us and generates those conceptual leaps of human fluid intelligence that can drive innovation. This capacity to see what is not obviously there is a genuine USP, given that by definition a system trained on existing data may see gaps in it like a missing shade of blue, but will struggle to invent new ideas or concepts.

One way we nurture this capacity is by fighting off the cognitive biases that curtail it. There are hundreds of models for defeating thinking traps, and creativity tools are legion. But just one model will serve to make the point about the mesmerising effect of data and the status quo as a mind-guard and limiting factor (see Box 7.3). Its author, Annette Moser-Wellman, identified five 'faces' through which innovation comes, and argues that creativity is our particular human gift and vocation, because creativity comes from the soul, and springs from a well of genius that is our ancient birth-right.[39] Some of these Faces would be readily achievable through AI, but the others illustrate the current frontiers, and talk to the puzzle of unfathomable human invention.

Her first Face is Seer, literally, one who sees. Such a person conjures up newness in their mind's eye, like the property developer who 'sees' the potential in an old ruin. JK Rowling talks of 'seeing' Harry Potter in the carriage one magic day as her train sped south: AI could now invent Harry Potter, because it could abstract new plots from existing stories, but could AI have invented Harry Potter from scratch?

Another Face is the Sage, a person who innovates by simplifying things, stripping them back to their essence. No-frills airlines have based their entire business model on this face. For AI, this path to innovation might be programmable, because it is about discerning what is essential. This could perhaps be achieved through analysing customer feedback, and data about costs: doing so, and removing one olive from the salad, famously saved American Airlines $40,000 a year.[40]

A third Face is the Observer, a person who innovates by noticing detail. When Richard Branson noticed that the worst part of a frequent flier's journey was the trip to the airport, he introduced a limo-bike service to speed passengers past traffic to the check-in desk on a chauffeured motorbike. Apple is also famous for attention to detail. When engaging the voice dictation feature on newer Mac laptops, Apple automatically slows the internal fan speed so it can better hear your voice. Smartphone convergence, contactless payment cards, and even loyalty-card key-rings use similar attention to detail to innovate. AI could absolutely do this, by tracking adverse feedback or effects and designing them out.

The fourth Face is that of the Alchemist. Alchemists create gold for businesses by mixing together ideas from different places. Doctors from Great Ormond Street Hospital called on the Ferrari and McLaren F1 teams to learn from the tight organisation of their pit crews. In analysing the handover from the operating theatre to Intensive Care, they managed to reduce errors by 40%. Interface carpets' biomimicry innovations are a further example of this kind of thinking, where Interface used the patterns of the forest floor to design modular tiling that could be laid in any combination, drastically reducing laying times and cost. This would require sophisticated programming, but I think AI could take this to the next level, by spotting patterns and opportunities for transfer that we simply cannot see.

Moser-Wellman's final face is that of the Fool. Innovation in this mode arises from the absurd, or by turning things upside down. When the London Metropolitan Police wanted to improve their arrest rates for robbery, someone made a joke about persuading burglars just to hand over their stolen goods. After his colleagues stopped laughing, they played around with the idea, and launched Operation Bumblebee: this increased their arrest rate because they worked closely with the pawn shops where burglars literally do hand over their stolen goods. This is a harder Face to translate. How could you safely program the absurd into AI?

Examining this creativity tool to see where it might suit AI serves to underscore the importance of the Sixth Sense in our human design. Apart from its capacity to supplement warning signals, it turns out that this junk code is particularly implicated in our ability to discover, innovate and improve the environment around us. Because of this, rather than discounting it as too ephemeral to matter, we need to recognise its power and seek to cultivate it.

Uncertainty

One way to describe the human ability to entertain uncertainty was another *bon mot* coined by the poet John Keats. Walking home from a Christmas pantomime in 1817, he was musing about the finest qualities of 'a man of achievement' like Shakespeare, and decided that the defining distinction was 'Negative Capability, that is, when a man is capable of being in uncertainties, mysteries, doubts, without any irritable reaching after fact and reason.'[41] Writing slightly later, Lewis Carroll puts his version of this into the mouth of the White Queen, when she meets Alice, through the looking glass:

> Alice laughed. 'There's no use trying,' she said. 'One can't believe impossible things.' 'I daresay you haven't had much practice,' said the Queen. 'When I was your age, I always did it for half-an-hour a day. Why, sometimes I've believed as many as six impossible things before breakfast.'[42]

This seeming foolishness is so important that it gave rise to Bayesian AI, because if AI cannot find a way to be uncertain it becomes unreliable. Humans are so good at it that there is a whole register for doubt, expressed in grammatical mood as the subjunctive. In linguistics, mood is split into two groups, realis and irrealis. Realis moods relate to things that are the case, whereas irrealis moods relate to things that are not the case, either because they will never be the case or because they are not yet the case. This means that realis moods are used to portray situations that are real – the kinds of things that are data – whereas irrealis moods are used to express things that exist in the realm of thought, that are known only through the imagination.[43] This distinction, between statements of fact and statements of possibility, has sometimes been shorthanded as the difference between assertion and non-assertion. But expressing something in an irrealis mood need not mean that the event or topic does not exist, rather it denotes on the part of the speaker a studied diffidence and conditionality. In English, the realis moods are the indicative (I believe) and the imperative (thou shalt), while the irrealis moods are the subjunctive (we might), the optative (I wish), and the interrogative (might we?).[44] This formal vocabulary for uncertainty shows how culturally salient it has always been, such that in most languages we have a particular set of word games devoted to it.

As we have seen in the discussion on metaphor and ambiguity in language, Iain McGilchrist would argue that this is a particular gifting of the brain's right hemisphere. While this has been culturally overshadowed since the Enlightenment and the ascendancy of science, it has recently been very much back in the spotlight because of the Covid-19 pandemic, when the existential experience of uncertainty was more globally shared than tends to be usual.

Interestingly it is the religions who are the global experts in inculcating good habits of uncertainty. Faith by definition requires a commitment to lifetime uncertainty, because no-one will know whether they are right or not until they are dead (and perhaps not even then). So the religions have developed a variety of routines to exercise this muscle. Some religions have taken this to extremes, and the much-pilloried woolliness of the Anglican church in the UK is a fine example. Ambiguity as a meta-competence is behind a principled inability ever to be too certain about anything. In Christianity, the central figure is somehow both God and man, dead and alive, historical and eternal. Entertaining the doctrine of the Trinity, which holds that God, Jesus, and the Holy Spirit are 'consubstantial and coeternal,' requires extraordinary mental agility; and the core texts, the four gospels, famously disagree with each other. To cope with holding these 'impossible things' in tension, religions tend to insist that faith be held up as a good thing in and of itself (see, for example, Martin Luther's emphasis on *sola fides*). Next, they use the routines of worship to feed confirmatory bias, rehearsing faith narratives week by week and year by year, as a perpetual reminder. Finally, they encourage believers to enact their faith in their everyday lives, the classic 'be and become' strategy. To help, they use role models to demonstrate the way. These may appear in the stories of holy books – whose re-telling is always a vital part of religious ritual – but are also retrieved from the centuries since, through the prophets and saints and other famous followers, many of whom enjoy dedicated memorials and feast days. Religion used to be so core to humanity's experience that we could rely on this training. In a secularising society, we need to build this formation back into the everyday to avoid this muscle atrophying, by taking the virtue of uncertainty seriously, and recognising this junk code as another of our superpowers.

As Bayesian AI has discovered, uncertainty is a vital tool for preventing error. It is having the courage to entertain the unknown, and to hang back from a premature and presumptive leap to conclusion. It also forces us to seek out other people, when we are unsure and need help, advice or leadership. This reduces risk by exposing ideas and decisions to the wisdom of crowds, as a way of testing them, and encourages humans to band together in communities. Our restless yearning for the resolution of uncertainty in order to restore control also acts as an impetus to solve problems which, in concert with the other elements of our junk code, drives improvement.

Free Will

For millennia, many tribes and people assumed they had no autonomy, and that life was being driven by the fates or by a predetermined design or creator. But ours is an era that luxuriates in free will. We have an existential fear of being programmed, and of waking up to find we have been someone's puppet all along. We dread the idea that all those times when we felt we were wrestling with our consciences or weighing up weighty arguments, the rules were already driving us towards a decision we had felt was our very own, and not one that had been preordained in someone else's playbook. If we have no agency, we have no freedom, except in an illusory and manipulative way.

The problem can be summarised by an extremely brief story penned by the SF writer Ted Chiang to demonstrate the perils of discovering life is pointless. The story is a warning about an imaginary device called a Predictor, which flashes if you press it. The problem is, it actually flashes one second before you press it, and is impossible to beat. Playing with it becomes addictive, and ultimately teaches you that there is no such thing as free will. In the story, humans accordingly lose the will to live.[45] This is the gamification of the observed phenomenon in neuroimaging that seems to show our choices originating in our brains before we even become aware of thinking about them. As the author Sam Harris puts it in his 2012 book *Free Will*, the science reveals us all to be 'biochemical puppets.'[46] This has led many scientists and philosophers to argue that free will is an illusion, which may have evolved as a way to make us experience our lives as meaningful.

Is this terminal? Cue Ted Chiang again, and another of his stories, which became the 2016 film *Arrival*.[47] In the story, a linguist learning an alien language gains access to an alien consciousness that knows the future. Unlike our consciousness, which runs from cause to effect and is sequential, theirs can see the whole arc of time simultaneously. Their life is about discerning purpose and enacting events, while ours is about discerning good outcomes and deploying our free will and volition to those ends. Chiang explains this theoretically with reference to Fermat's principle of least time. This states that the path taken by a ray between two given points is the path that can be traversed in the least time. Lurking behind this idea is the realisation that nature has an ability to test alternative paths: a ray of sunlight must know its destination in order to choose the optimal route. Chiang has his protagonist muse about the nature of free will in such a scheme: the virtue would not be in selecting the right actions, but in duly performing already known actions, in order that the future occurs as it should. This would be a bit like an actor respecting Shakespeare enough not to improvise one of his soliloquies. So our lives would still be full of meaning and choice, but of a different type. Elsewhere this has been drawn as the difference between determinism and fatalism: you may have been dealt a certain hand of cards, but how you play them is not a foregone conclusion: your choices still matter, and will have consequences. So were free will as we experience it not to exist in fact, there would still be a need for ethics. Perhaps instead of utilitarianism, the philosophies in vogue would need to be behavioural ethics like virtue ethics and Stoicism. As Wittgenstein puts it, 'if we take eternity to mean not infinite temporal duration but timelessness, then eternal life belongs to those who live in the present.'[48]

We have already looked briefly at Free Will in the context of whether or not the law could operate if it could be proven that there was no such thing. But in the context of our junk code, the crucial element seems to be our *perception* of having free will: in spite of fashions throughout history, notably in the Christian doctrine of predestination, humans seem to cling to a belief that they have genuine agency and choice. This seems to be a definitional property of humanity, without which we feel *dehumanised*. Which is why imprisonment and the withdrawal of ordinary freedoms is used by society as a punishment. Those writing most movingly about incarceration make the point, like Victor Frankl in *Man's Search for Meaning*, that an ability to find ways to keep feeling free is vital to human survival.[49]

Precision about perception over reality risks an approach that divorces the two, but of course the perception of free will cannot endure in the face of a sustained lack of it in reality. But it does help to focus in on the mental activity involved. A key feature of consciousness has been described by Tegmark as our ability to notice our own processing, so volition is experienced as that sense that we can process at will. It would therefore be true that if we became aware of our own programming as a species and discovered rules governing our every decision, we would become aware of our design limitations and no longer feel 'free.' This is why the SF writers think that such a discovery would effectively switch us off. Because, when examined as a core part of our junk code, it becomes obvious that Free Will is its animator. While tempered by uncertainty and thwarted by mistakes, it is fuelled by emotions and our Sixth Sense, and our stories are all about deriving meaning from examples of our agency. Our felt sense of volition is vital to our ability to make plans, to discover and to be creative, because it allows us to imagine that the future is not fixed. If we thought it was, there would be no incentive to improve. This is the heart of our difference and distinctiveness: we are the 'un-programmed.' While we might borrow teleologies as both explanations and motivators, we do so secure in knowing that we do not have any pre-set teleology that controls our destiny. Free will is therefore both the cornerstone and the stumbling block of human design.

Meaning

The psychologist Steven Pinker thinks that the biggest breakthrough of the scientific revolution was 'to nullify the intuition that the universe is saturated with purpose.'[50] It is a popular move for the ultra-scientific to denigrate humanity's addiction to meaning-making. Famously, in the popular film The Matrix it is this flaw that enables our alien overlords to farm us efficiently. But the accelerating mental health crisis does rather prove that the exercise of this capacity is hardwired into our ability to thrive.

It was the psychologist Oliver James who introduced the concept of 'affluenza' into the lexicon through his 2007 book.[51] He argued that the contagion of the affluenza 'virus' in the West, bringing unprecedented emotional distress, is caused by modern capitalism. He argues that affluenza is essentially the curse of meaninglessness, or what the ancient Greeks would call acedia, or soul-sickness. Thomas Aquinas called acedia 'the sorrow of the world' and, while James and Layard would blame capitalism, history would suggest that it is just the latest culprit in a story that is as old as time: whenever humans feel purposeless, they feel sad.

So, in response to the finding that, on average, people have grown no happier in the last 50 years – despite average incomes more than doubling – the economist Richard Layard set about trying to establish what truly makes us happy. Certainly there is a ceiling of $20,000 annual income after which happiness is not materially altered.[52] Layard opts for a definition of happiness as 'feeling good,' such that in normal circumstances we will gravitate towards things that make us feel good and away from things that do not.[53] Using data from the World Values Survey, the US General Social Survey and many others, he has established seven Factors that affect happiness, with the first five being in order of priority (see Box 7.4).[54]

As in most happiness studies, Layard's top factor is family relationships. These have the highest valency, particularly when they change. Indeed, it is change to any of these factors that most affects happiness, both positively and negatively, but base levels of means, health, and community are key anchors, held within a frame of personal values. It is this final happiness factor, arising from personal values or a philosophy of life, that most helps to avoid affluenza, because it provides a framework for making life feel

BOX 7.4 LAYARD'S 7 FACTORS AFFECTING HAPPINESS

1. Family relationships
2. Financial situation
3. Work
4. Community and friends
5. Health
6. Personal freedom
7. Personal values

purposeful. The strongest correlation is between happiness and belief in God, although this factor includes any commitment to an explicit philosophy of life.[55] This is important because a belief system provides an internal barometer of value. Solely external goals and motives only increase vulnerability to boredom, depression, anxiety and personality disorder.[56]

One aspect of that explicit philosophy seems to need to be about humanity's cosmic significance. A 2021 study examined whether or not social mattering was the same as cosmic mattering in the ability of religion to provide the meaning of life. Overwhelmingly it was this need to matter at a cosmic level that was more salient.[57] This would cohere with psychologist Richard Beck's thesis about the role in positive mental health of a feeling of 'enchantment.' He argues that we have gone off transcendence because, a bit like shying away from trusting authority, we are now not keen on the idea that there might be anything or anyone 'over and above' us. That feels very parental, and implies judgement and critique, so it makes us feel childish.[58] But the psychological risk of there being no dimension other than the one we are in, is that we start to feel trapped by the echo-chamber, limited by the predictability of the already known. Is that really it, when we have bought everything we can possibly buy, visited everywhere we possibly can, and had every experience we have ever heard of? That is when humans experience what he calls 'The Ache' and feel sad.[59] A sense of there being 'something else' must be more important than we had supposed, because the loss of it societally seems to have reduced mental health and not improved it. When it is hard to find hope in other people, whose flaws may be the reason for our predicament, a sense of the transcendent – or what Beck would call 'enchantment' – becomes vital to our will to survive, as has been attested to in many a grim story about incarceration. In these situations, even a lack of freedom can be compensated for by a strong sense of hope, because of a sense of meaning and purpose.[60]

Religion as a particular type of meaning-making seems to be a very persistent bug in our programming. While the World Values Survey would suggest that this has waned with affluence, and particularly so over the last decade,[61] 2019 research by Pew shows that a global average of 62% still say that religion plays an important role in their lives.[62] This varies a lot by culture and geography, and even the rising 'Nones' in the US and UK populations are not always without faith, many have just rejected institutionalised religion.[63] But the blip in the data after the collapse of the Soviet Union, even if it has since corrected, is a reminder that humans still turn to religion when their world has turned upside down. This may be considered a misplaced homing instinct to modern secular eyes, but it is a phenomenon that begs a question. As we have seen, the function of religion in the defence and resilience of our junk code should not be underestimated, and will certainly need to be replicated if not in an exclusively religious context.

COMMUNITY

Is it possible to read back from these capabilities into the underlying source code? There is certainly a pattern behind them. For centuries philosophers, theologians and storytellers have tried to fathom why any creator would award such a wayward creation free will. The existence of the rest of the junk code is why so many have argued that free will must be an illusion, because otherwise as a species we have been set up to fail; and if we were created by a benevolent life-force this act of sabotage makes no sense. If free will is the price of allowing us to experience our lives as meaningful, it seems too high a price to pay. But if – as we have with AI – you have this choice to make, how might you try to safeguard your vulnerable creatures, so that this gift of volition does not destroy them? Well, you include alongside that gift a whole raft of stabilising influences by way of risk mitigation. This, to me, means that what we had dismissed as Junk Code turns out to be the best clue we have for understanding the source code of soul.

Evolution teaches us that if the aim is survival, learning and adaptation must be the superpower; and in humans it seems that this is particularly facilitated by our junk code. Because looking afresh at it, we can trace through it something that resembles a suite of ameliorators, sharing a common theme: they all locate us within a community in order that there might be safety in numbers. For instance, our emotions are there to help us relate better in relationship. Apart from self-regulation, they have limited use for someone living in isolation, but as a functionality they are vital to promote healthy community living. Next up, our accident-prone nature, which helps us develop both a conscience to avoid mistakes that create harm, and skills in preparation for when we do make mistakes. This propensity for error makes us naturally seek others for guidance, counsel and comfort. This homing instinct for community we can now see as a regulating mechanism, to limit damage and to share learning for the benefit of the whole. We then consolidate this through storytelling, which at heart is about cementing identity and transmitting life-lessons, again in community. Indeed, we use our emotions to tag our stories, so that we can retell them complete with their original emotional soundtrack.[64] Intuition is harder to assign, because it is such a disputed concept, but wherever it comes from, it seems to allow us to access knowledge that otherwise seems to dwell in the realm of the collective unconscious: again, drawing on the wisdom of communities both of the present and the past. And uncertainty? Because we find it uncomfortable, we gravitate towards leaders who might help us navigate our way through the fog, which again forms us into communities.

All of these lines of 'junk' code promote co-operation, and the kind of reciprocal altruism and sense of mattering that creates sustainable communities over time. For humans, existence is not a solitary journey. Even before we knew who we were, we had already benefitted from belonging. We are the inheritors of all the practices and institutions that our forebears created for us: tribe, family, health, education, law. We are designed to be humans in relationship.[65] And given that our design has carefully included and retained all this misunderstood code, perhaps we should take it more seriously?

NOTES

1 McEwan, Ian (2020) *Machines Like Me*, London: Vintage, p149.
2 With apologies and due acknowledgement to those whose health has removed their sense of volition, and to those who yearn to feel free.
3 See Martinón-Torres, M, d'Errico, F, Santos, E et al (2021) 'Earliest known human burial in Africa,' *Nature* 593, p95–100 at https://www.nature.com/articles/s41586-021-03457-8.
4 Larkin, Philip (1964) *The Whitsun Weddings*, London: Faber & Faber, the poem 'An Arundel Tomb,' p46.
5 Another more recent study identified 27 universal emotions, but omitted several of Ekman's, like anger and guilt. Since these seem to me to be such obvious universal emotions, I am using Ekman's older list, particularly given that most of those in the longer list would also map to his 'families,' or be what he would instead call moods. But for completeness, see the study by Berkeley's Cowen and Keltner here: https://www.pnas.org/content/114/38/E7900.

6   I am excluding sex from my list of Junk Code because it does not fit there. I am aware that there is much debate in AI about sexbots, so this may seem negligent. But in this context it is not a distinctively *human* proclivity or activity, in spite of our ability to make a particular feature of it in the human experience.

7   See Table 3.1 in Ekman, Paul (1999), 'Basic emotions,' in Dalgleish, T & Power, M, eds, *Handbook of Cognition and Emotion*, Chichester: Wiley, p56.

8   Goleman, Daniel (1996) *Emotional Intelligence*, London: Bloomsbury, p14f. For a more general explanation of the brain and emotions, see McGilchrist, Iain (2009) *The Master and His Emissary*, New Haven, CT: Yale University Press, p58–64.

9   As coined in Schulz, Kathryn (2010) *Being Wrong*, London: Granta, p10.

10 Ariely, Dan (2009) *Predicably Irrational*, London: Harper.

11 Kahneman, Daniel (2012) *Thinking Fast and Slow*, London: Penguin.

12 Which stands for the Human Propensity to Fuck things Up, see Spufford, Francis (2012) *Unapologetic*, London: Faber & Faber, p27f.

13 Ibid., p49.

14 The human tendency to lie deserves a separate inquiry, for which the recommended starting point is still the classic treatment by Bok, Sissela (1999) *Lying*, New York: Vintage. How to teach 'truth' to AI is already a pressing question in an era of fake news and algorithmic bias – and whose truth - and is one of the key debates in the field of machine ethics.

15 Guiso, Luigi, Sapienza, Paola & Zingales, Luigi (2003) 'People's opium? Religion and economic attitudes,' *Journal of Monetary Economics*, 50:1, p225–282.

16 See the discussion on Kierkegaard in Bash, Anthony (2020) *Remorse*, Eugene, OR: Cascade, p1f and footnotes.

17 Ibid., p222 and throughout.

18 Keats, John (2009) *Selected Letters*, Oxford: OUP, p232.

19 Hick, John (1991) *Evil and the God of Love*, Basingstoke: Macmillan, p256.

20 Writers like CS Lewis have called this junk code conscience. For him, the innate 'moral law' that tries to prompt us to behave well is the closest we can get to understanding the mind that programmed us. But calling this 'conscience' tends to descend into a discussion about how to code in (whose) morality. The field of machine ethics is fraught because, as the COMEST report puts it 'there are no definitive philosophical answers to questions about the nature of morality itself, and about the objectivity or subjectivity of ethical frameworks themselves' (see paragraph 199 on p45, at https://unesdoc. unesco.org/ark:/48223/pf0000253952). I have therefore stuck to mistakes and remorse which I think are the more precise signs of human soul. See Lewis, CS (2002) *Mere Christianity*, London: Harper Collins, pp3–32.

21 Booker, Christopher (2004) *The Seven Basic Plots*, London: Continuum, p7.

22 Ibid., p10.

23 See Papadopoulos, Renos K, ed (2006) *The Handbook of Jungian Psychology*, London: Routledge. For an unusual literary foray into this territory see *The Manticore*, the second book of Davies, Robertson (1983) *The Deptford Trilogy*, London: Penguin, p447–451.

24 See in particular his commentary p555–558 in Booker, Christopher (2004) *The Seven Basic Plots*, London: Continuum.

25 Ibid., p692.

26 Ibid., p573f.

27 See Tolkien, JRR (2009) *Tree and Leaf*, London: HarperCollins, pp68ff. With thanks to Richard Beck for pointing out this essay and the concept of eucatastrophe.

28 Gladwell, Malcolm (2006) *Blink*, London: Penguin.

29 Kahneman, Daniel (2012) *Thinking, Fast and Slow*, London: Penguin.

30 Hume, David (1999) *An Enquiry Concerning Human Understanding*, Oxford: OUP in 'Of the Origin of Ideas' (Section 2:8), p98f.

31 An invention for which she was finally recognised in 1997 with the Electronic Frontier Foundation Pioneer Award and the Invention Convention's BULBIE Gnass Spirit of Achievement Award, and in 1998 the Viktor Kaplan Medal of the Austrian Association of Patent Holders and Inventors. See Rhodes, Richard (2012) *Hedy's Folly*, New York: Vintage, p214–218.

32 See section II:xi in Wittgenstein, Ludwig (1958) *Philosophical Investigations*, trans Anscombe, GEM, Oxford: Blackwell, pp193ff.

33 Commentators have noted Wittgenstein's use of the word Aufleuchten here, which has been variously translated as the 'dawning' or 'lighting up' of an aspect.

34 Wittgenstein, Ludwig (1958) *Philosophical Investigations*, trans Anscombe, GEM, Oxford: Blackwell, p197; p212.

35 In Neal Stephenson's book *Anathem* he depicts this quale as an 'upsight,' which he defines as a sudden, usually unlooked for moment of clear understanding. Stephenson, Neal (2008) *Anathem*, London: Atlantic, p952.

36 Coleridge, ST (1997) *The Complete Poems of Samuel Taylor Coleridge*, London: Penguin, p250.

37 Millbank, Paul (2022) 'A society without imagination: a lament,' *The Kenarchy Journal*, 3, p1, at https://kenarchy.org/starting-points-health-and-wellbeing/.

38 Ibid., p5.

39 Moser-Wellman, Annette (2002) *Five Faces of Genius*, New York: Penguin.

40 See https://www.forbes.com/sites/moiravetter/2015/06/04/the-40000-olive-how-entrepreneurs-can-spend-time-saving-money/?sh=1e89540b5fbb.

41 See the 21–27 December 1817 letter to his brothers George and Tom, in Keats, John (2009) *Selected Letters*, Oxford: OUP, p41f.

42 Carroll, Lewis (1910) *Through the Looking Glass and What Alice Found There*, London: Macmillan, p101.

43 Palmer, FR (2001): *Mood and Modality*, Cambridge: CUP, p1f and pp145ff.

44 Palmer, FR (1973): *Grammar*, Harmondsworth: Pelican, p83.

45 See 'What's Expected of Us,' in Chiang, Ted (2019) *Exhalation*, London: Picador, pp58–61.

46 Harris, Sam (2012) *Free Will*, New York: Free Press, p47; and see the general overview and discussion of brain tumours in https://www.theguardian.com/news/2021/apr/27/the-clockwork-universe-is-free-will-an-illusion.

47 See 'Story of Your Life,' in Chiang, Ted (2002) *Stories of Your Life and Others*, London: Picador, p111–172.

48 Wittgenstein, Ludwig (2016) *Tractatus Logico-Philosophicus*, trans Ogden, CK, Asheville, NC: Chiron Academic Press, 6:4311, p88.

49 Frankl, Viktor E (2004) *Man's Search for Meaning*, London: Rider.

50 As quoted in Foster, Charles (2021) *Being A Human*, London: Profile, p314; see his comments on the 2017 Edge question here: https://www.edge.org/response-detail/27023.

51 James, Oliver (2007) *Affluenza*, London: Vermillion.

52 Layard, Richard (2005) *Happiness*, London: Penguin, p33 (same page in 2011 edition).

53 Ibid., p12.

54 Ibid., p63.

55 Ibid., p71f.

56 James, Oliver (2008) *The Selfish Capitalist*, London: Vermillion, p71.

57 Prinzing, M, Van Cappellen, P, & Fredrickson, BL (2021) 'More than a momentary blip in the universe?' *Personality and Social Psychology Bulletin*, at https://doi.org/10.1177/01461672211060136.

58 Beck, Richard (2021) *Hunting Magic Eels*, Minneapolis, MN: Broadleaf, p212f.

59 Ibid., p8.

60 Ibid., p98f.

61 The World Values Survey shows an increase in religious belief between 1981 and 2007 post-Communism, then a rapid decline between 2007 and 2020, in line with rising affluence. See Inglehart, Ronald F (2021) *Religion's Sudden Decline: What's Causing It, and What Comes Next?* New York: OUP.

62 See https://www.pewresearch.org/global/2020/07/20/the-global-god-divide/

63 See Woodhead, LJP (2016) 'The Rise of 'No Religion' in Britain: the emergence of a new cultural majority', *Journal of the British Academy*, 4, p245–261.

64 A fascinating study has shown that the emotional freight of a story is preserved through multiple retellings of it, whether or not it is lengthened or condensed, which suggests we use the emotional soundtrack of a story as a heuristic to remember them, see Breithaupt, Fritz, Li, Binyan & Kruschke, John (2022) 'Serial reproduction of narratives preserves emotional appraisals,' *Cognition and Emotion* 15, p1–21.

65 For a similar conclusion reached via an argument about *imago dei*, see Dorobantu, Marius (2021) 'Cognitive vulnerability, artificial intelligence, and the image of god in humans', *Journal of Disability & Religion*, 25:1, p27–40.

CHAPTER 8

Cultivating Soul

When I consider thy heavens, the work of thy fingers, the moon and the stars, which thou hast ordained; What is man, that thou art mindful of him? and the son of man, that thou visitest him?

Psalm 8:3–4

The neurophysiologists will one day give us their full account, which will itself be reducible to a set of chemical and finally of physical explanations. But will such an account give us what we want?

Alasdair MacIntyre, The Unconscious *(1958)*

CULTIVATING JUNK CODE

This analysis of humanity's Junk Code collectively points towards our overwhelming need to matter, both to ourselves and to others. Our coding drives us into community, because reciprocal mattering generates sustainable communities and the flourishing of our species as a whole. But this need to feel as though we matter both to ourselves and others suggests that ultimately we may need to feel as though we matter to AI. However, unless or until their programming includes emotion or nostalgia, we could only make a rational case to AI for our future survival. Given that we have designed them to have superior intelligence, the case would have to be a compelling one. So we should use the story of our neglected code to make the case for our utility as a species, but we should also role model these human values as training data for AI.

DOI: 10.1201/9781003366614-8

To recap, the collective effect of our junk code is to encourage us into relationship. The seven elements work together in a synchronised way to promote this. First, emotion provides the feelings we need to tell if we matter or not. Excellence at picking up these signals and trusting them then helps us tune our antennae to discern information from our Sixth Sense too. And this data helps us calibrate our use of free will, particularly when we are uncertain about what to do. When we inevitably make mistakes, our emotions guide us towards reparation, in order that we might matter rightly again. Throughout our lives, our stories and our yearning for meaning drive us towards the discovery of an ever deeper purpose, and this – hopefully – convinces us that we finally matter. So what might we do to strengthen each of these strands of code so that we might demonstrate them more fully in our lives?

Emotions

Daniel Goleman's 1995 classic *Emotional Intelligence* was on the best-seller lists for over a year and translated into over 40 languages, but it was not until this century that its message started to be internalised in the everyday imagination, and promoted in education. He was the first to argue the popular case for the emotions to be considered as a material phenomenon and not just a concept. In the years since, there have been multiple attempts to take seriously the need not only to recognise the important role of emotions but also how best to school them. In the educational curricula this ranges from nursery children drawing faces on teddy bear templates by way of 'mood reviews,' to business executives completing psychometrics designed to measure their levels of emotional competence.

One intriguing development has been an initiative pioneered by the neuroscientist Patricia Riddell with Eton College about teaching teenagers about their own brain development, given that the development of the risk and reward receptors is asymmetric in puberty, and differs by gender. This has major implications for their own emotional development, and for public policy directed at this particular age group.[1] Standardising emotional education throughout primary, secondary, and tertiary/professional curricula should therefore continue at pace to help everyone feel able to enjoy and deploy their emotions well. This also means that fields of inquiry into the neurodiverse must re-articulate the role of the emotions, not as an ableist reproach but as a narrative about our species that must be taken seriously. Demonstrating through public policy that our emotions matter, and are not imagined or irrational or weak or silly should be a default and not a fad.

More generally, our emotions are implicated in our ability to experience qualia as a feature of consciousness, and as such any attempt to strengthen our emotional code should school us in qualia too. This argues in favour of public policy concerning green spaces, leisure, art, music, sport, and heritage, as well as educational initiatives involving these things, because we should wallow in our ability to appreciate the sensory world. During the various pandemic lockdowns, it was notable how much solace people found in nature and birdsong, and how much being a part of nature made them feel as though they mattered. While AI may learn its own version of consciousness in the future, this is uniquely ours at present, and we should actively cherish it.

Mistakes

There are a variety of ways in which we can help humans both to understand this code and to hone it appropriately. Obviously there should be no intention to encourage humans to relish mistake-making to the extent that it becomes pathological. So with the caveat that 'normal' formation is supposed to provide enough education to reduce stupidity, what should be the focus on this way of mattering? As we have seen, the area of mistake-making encourages a degree of humility which compels humans into community. In particular, the development of conscience drives the need for morality and character, and an instinct for reparation. Because an underlying worldview or code of ethics is vital for underpinning Free Will, morality will be discussed in that context.

Meanwhile, the surest way to equip humans to deal with mistakes is to attend to the formal development of character. The educationalist Kurt Hahn pioneered character education in the 1930s both in Germany and in the UK, giving birth to a range of global movements and initiatives that prioritise the development of character in their pedagogy. Using one of his schools as a testing ground, in 2015 Simon Beames and his team set about defining the essence of character education, interviewing both current pupils and their parents, and former pupils over many generations, in order to track the stickiness of the 'character' developed.[2] Their findings can be summarised under five headings:[3]

(1) Learning to try
    Formal learning should include a varied and repeated out-of-classroom curriculum. This must be compulsory for all students, in order to compel them to try things they would otherwise avoid,

ranging from music and drama to adventure and sport. This may require ingenuity or extra resourcing, to avoid those with more money being able to 'buy' these experiences at the expense of those less well off. The Beames research showed that the resultant 'have a go' mentality lasts well beyond school, and had inspired those involved to keep trying new things for the rest of their lives.

(2) Learning to fail

Making the out-of-classroom curriculum compulsory means that some degree of failure is inevitable for everyone, given that it is unlikely that everyone will be good at everything. This means that, by design, students learn to fail, and they learn that others fail too. They learn that they may need other people to succeed, but also that they may be better than others at unexpected things. The reason these opportunities should be offered 'out of the classroom' is so that they remain unexamined. This lack of a formal test environment provides the necessary opportunity for experimentation, and creates a safe environment where failure is not considered socially or educationally terminal.

(3) Learning to try again

Because such a character curriculum would be regular and repeated, students have to have another go at things, even if they failed last time. So they learn resilience, and about conquering their fears both about their own abilities, and about how their peers will react to them. Again, this teaches students how to pick themselves up. Many of the alumni involved in the Beames research reported that this ability to bounce back had been crucial in helping them to navigate subsequent setbacks. This suggests that students must be given opportunities both to identify their fears and to set about conquering them, whether it is public speaking, a fear of heights or water, or just plain social shyness.

(4) Social levelling

Because Gordonstoun, the school used in the study, was designed by Hahn to mix the social classes and to bring together children from all over the world, this particular research revealed a useful insight about the wider social benefits of character education, as a tool both for social levelling and for teaching humility: it does not matter who your parents are or where you come from if you are the one who has forgotten to pack snacks when your team is out camping. Students had often found themselves being led or rescued by peers they would never have expected to thrive in these contexts, so this kind of character education engenders a humility and respect for other people based on ability and character, and not on culture or background. This learning can be designed into any group context, by exposing the same group of people to a range of contexts, where different people will have a chance to shine each time.

(5) Gender

While gender is understood to be more complex these days, for the women involved in the Beames research, being pitted against men in so many different environments had instilled a particularly steady career confidence. Working together both inside and outside, they had seen men be worse as well as better than them in a wide variety of contexts. This shaped their expectations in the workplace, which had helped the alumnae to thrive. In the same way that character education can be a social leveller, it can therefore help to address gender bias and stereotypes. While this research sample did not collect demographics about neurodiversity or physical ability, thoroughly mixed groups that have to learn interdependence in safe educational settings are more likely to be able to replicate this in their wider social environment as adults.

The boarding school used for this research is of a particular type, but the nature of these findings has obvious transfer to educational environments right across the age range. It challenges the narrowing of educational policy in many geographies to focus on academic achievement, and the well-meaning culture in many countries that tries to protect children from failing.

But if you do fail, in spite of your best efforts, a human is hard-wired to feel bad about it. This emotion is known as remorse, although there is a spectrum of emotion about mistakes that includes regret, ruefulness and chagrin. Remorse in particular tends to generate an orientation towards reparation and, as we have seen from the work of Anthony Bash, these feelings are metabolised through acts of repentance, which is when they become particularly societally salient. In order to feel as though we matter, we need to be able not only to recover from setbacks through strength of character, but also to prove we still matter to those we have wronged by making reparation.

Our grounding in Emotional Intelligence and character should give us the skills to do this well, but given its pivotal role in community repair, reparation should also be foregrounded in public policy. In many juris-dictions, there has been a shift to a penal code that takes restitution more seriously as a formal response to wrong-doing. This is often a pragmatic move to reduce incarceration volumes, but if well-designed is about both the rehabilitation of the offender and about 'making good' the harm they have caused the community in some suitable way. Making a teenager clean up their own graffiti may seem a paltry response, but through a moral lens it is about teaching consequences and building character, and doing both in public.

Storytelling

Scheherazade told tales for 1,001 nights. Most children could do this too, even if it was just endless versions of their very favourite bed-time story. They are so instinctive about stories, that they can immediately spot one that is 'wrong.' But as adults we seem to have had our capacity for spinning yarns schooled out of us. Fiction is still a vibrant and ever-growing literary category, but funding for the arts continues to be squeezed in many areas in the world, because it is deemed a luxury. Our argument about junk code would suggest that this policy should be reversed. It may be too much to expect adults to re-join story-circles if they are not obliged to attend them as parents or grandparents, but a vibrant cultural scene keeps stories alive through film, theatre and performance, both in permanent arts venues and through festivals and awards. Public libraries and public broadcasting are vital to this effort, to ensure that everyone gets access to stories, not just the privileged and wealthy; but again there needs to be a reverse in public spending policy to safeguard these vital assets. Books for children through schools and other charities are crucial, as are the efforts being made through various oral history initiatives to collect the stories of our elderly before they disappear completely. Stories teach us about who we are, so the more storytelling there is, the more we feel as though we have a place in the world.

Sixth Sense

Resourcefulness is another key way in which we contribute to the com-munities in which we live. One of our neglected resources is our Sixth Sense, long-discounted as imagination, hysteria or witchcraft. As we have seen, this capacity is almost certainly there to supplement our datasets, so we should take it seriously. It appears that our Sixth Sense is a com-bination of information from our subconscious, impressions from our environment, and the classic Sixth Sense 'gut feel' from the collective unconscious. Priming our Emotional Intelligence should help us learn to trust these kinds of impressions and instincts. Second Sight was one name given to an eerie ability to sense things that others could not. It was one of the signs of 'witchcraft' that saw so many women in the West in the Early Modern period hunted, burned or drowned. Recent moves in countries like Scotland[4] to pardon the witches should be part of a wider attempt to understand the gifting of those who seem to have heightened access to our Sixth Sense, in the same way that the neurodiverse often have heightened access to other capabilities.

Uncertainty

It is a good time to be writing about uncertainty. In the academic world it has burgeoned in popularity as a topic in a wide variety of disciplines, not just in maths and economics, but increasingly in the world of business strategy, psychology and leadership. In terms of how humans tend to feel about it, due to the ascendancy of the left hemisphere, Iain McGilchrist would argue that we have learned to fear it, and to yearn instead for the control that certainty gives us. This is reflected in voting patterns in times of tribulation, where we are more likely to favour a leader who is certain, even if they are extreme, than one who is more nuanced in their perspective. But the Covid-19 pandemic gave the whole world a masterclass in uncertainty. And it certainly was uncomfortable. But could one of the legacies of this grim period be a sensitisation to uncertainty that we could inculcate? As we have seen, uncertainty drives us into the arms of our fellow humans and encourages community. It makes us matter to others when we can be the remedy for their uncertainty, because it offers us an opportunity to be helpful.

The problem about cultivating uncertainty today is that there has recently been a formal shift away from it. We have heard McGilchrist's take on why, but the effect in educational policy has been a move at both school and university towards specific and vociferous support for STEM: Science, Technology, Engineering and Mathematics. This looks at first blush like a very sensible strategy, particularly when fused with initiatives to attract women into these male-dominated disciplines, and is about favouring concrete and 'useful' disciplines over those that feel more luxurious and self-indulgent. But when, in an attempt to discover whether better levels of education would reduce a tendency for people to be attracted to terrorism, the British Council found to the contrary that terrorists tend to be highly qualified already, and particularly in STEM subjects. A 2007 study by Gambetta and Hertog, later published as *Engineers of Jihad*, found that almost half of all known jihadis were university graduates, 44% of which had studied engineering. In the group more widely, there was a general bias towards technical subjects, which may explain why subjects like law, political science and philosophy are often banned from the universities in extremist regimes.[5] Why does this matter? Because the alluring black-and-white mindset, reinforced by the way STEM subjects are taught and examined, is morally problematic. It drives out opinion and debate, in an area when there can only be one right answer. Uncertainty thrives in areas where there could be a whole range of perspectives and possibilities. Nurturing this muscle is a strong argument for a policy correction in favour of 'woolly' subjects like philosophy and the arts, that require argument and exactly this kind of mental agility. The ethicist Nigel Biggar has argued that this is why the Humanities subjects have such a vital role to play in the moral formation of discernment and good choosing, because, unlike the more quantitative subjects, they require the development of sophisticated reasoning, and the ability to make compelling arguments about qualitative matters.[6] While AI can already match and indeed beat us on STEM, we will be ahead on this capacity for uncertainty and nuance if only we keep deliberately entertaining it, and not designing it out of our classrooms and lecture-halls.

There is a small but important example of how we are literally editing out uncertainty. In English, children are now taught that using the passive voice is bad grammar, and that they must use the active voice instead, in order to avoid ambiguity: 'Eve made mistakes' is better than 'mistakes were made.' But some of our greatest works of literature and rhetoric make excellent use of this device precisely in order to make a virtue of just that ambiguity: 'If it were done when 'tis done, then 'twere well it were done quickly …' So we should teach the passive to children, and show them how to use it well.

Free Will

We have established that the *feeling* of free will is arguably more important than the reality of it, because it is that felt sense of volition and agency that drives meaning-making, purpose and positive mental health. While we should continue to protect the actuality of human free will, by defending freedoms globally through conventions like the Universal Declaration on Human Rights, we should also attend to the perception of free will in the public imagination. This does involve a curmudgeonly attack on the use of statistics in journalism. These are usually bandied around in service of nudging a positive statement over the line, into an argument that something should either be normative or that it is somehow inevitable: crime figures are up, kids spend six hours a day on screens, and there are now more foodbanks than branches of Iceland. But the subliminal effect of being told that we are all predictable is to make us feel less free.

And paradoxically, we may also need to narrow our options in order to promote a real sense of choice. In 2000, Columbia's Sheena Iyengar conducted a famous jam experiment as an illustration of how too much choice paralyses consumers. In the experiment, she compared the behaviour of shoppers offered a choice of 24 jams, and those offered just six. Both groups were given coupons for a subsequent purchase. Those exposed to the larger selection seemed confused by the array of options, and tended to leave the shop empty-handed. While 30% of customers offered the smaller selection bought jam, only 3% of those offered the larger selection did so.[7] This befuddlement in the face of a welter of options is often why people feel impotent, and end up defaulting to the familiar or succumbing to peer pressure.

In parallel, we must equip our children with the tools they need to make good use of their free will through excellent choosing. This is a mixture of acquiring the good habits of virtue ethics and character, whichever wisdom tradition you select as a guide, and equipping people to choose a worldview to steer their choices, religious or otherwise. Once you have the right habits and the right rules, it becomes easier to navigate the sheer volume of dilemmas and options which are presented to us every day of our lives. If we fail in this task, people are rudderless, and subject to the magnetic force of celebrities and the powerful, who do not always make the best role models. René Girard would argue that this is because our default is to copy. His 1961 theory of 'mimetic desire' argues that we learn by copying not just the behaviour of those that surround us, but also their desires. This means that in the absence of any ideas of our own, we will drift into doing whatever the next person is doing, particularly if we want to impress them or compete with them. This leads to manipulation and group think, which ends up reducing our volition, so we become less able over time to realise and exercise our own agency. Consumerism is a mighty foe in this regard, and it takes a concerted effort to equip citizens with the strength to resist such strong and consistent messaging, particularly now that it has harnessed the might of AI and our smartphones.[8]

This is why Richard Layard includes philosophical and religious ideas in his Curriculum for Happiness. He thinks that an integrative curriculum in primary schools would include: understanding and managing your feelings (including anger and rivalry); loving and serving others (including practical exercises and learning about role models); the appreciation of beauty; causes and cures of illness, including mental illness, drugs and alcohol; love, family and parenting; work and money; understanding the media and preserving your own values; understanding others and how to socialise; political participation; and philosophical and religious ideas. The curriculum should also include physical exercise and music and art.[9]

But including anything that looks like worldviews in the school curriculum has become so culturally complex that it is quietly being dropped, except in the faith schools, or in formal examined courses in religion and philosophy. While it would no longer be appropriate to focus on one religion to the exclusion of all others, it is foolish to ignore them all just because the area is challenging; and even more foolish to avoid philosophy altogether. So I would argue for an urgent review, to design curricula that are broad enough to expose children to a range of global world views, but deep enough for them to locate themselves in one of them. Even secularism is a worldview, and it is duplicitous not to reveal this. Apart from assisting pragmatically with free will through decision-making, these frameworks are vital for our final piece of underestimated code, Meaning.

Meaning

Accumulatively, these moves should protect and enhance our ability to experience life as meaningful, because they would make us feel as though we matter. We matter because we are special. Our calling is to fulfil our special design as humans and to flourish as the kind of creatures that we are, not to attempt longingly to be something else or better.[10] That is why we must be the very best versions of ourselves that we can be. We may not understand the complexities of our source code or why it is there, but it gives us an extraordinary ability to self-determine in a way that a robot can never truthfully do. The blessing of free will is girded about with helpful instincts that allow us to entertain uncertainty, to be alive to our Sixth Sense, to deploy our emotions, and even to make mistakes. AI does not have that freedom. We reinforce and communicate our learning through storytelling and our endless capacity to make meaning of the world around us, and there is no other species that has ever emerged with such an extraordinary set of capabilities.

The rediscovery and promotion of the importance of philosophies of life will help to provide a formal frame for the meaning of the human experience. This may require a less dismissive tone from the commentators about religion, given how important an explanatory framework it is for so many people. Paradoxically, modern efforts to define the soul in the context of workplace spirituality have often been decried for being artificially denuded of any religious or deeper meaning, but in the context of our inquiry into junk code, their definitions of spirituality are spot on. As we saw, these cohere around concepts like purpose, values, meaning-making, being good or ethical, connectedness, transcendence, self-actualisation, and other-worldliness.[11] We can recognise this as a deracinated version of the soul as described by Plato and Descartes, but one that hones in on our particularity in the context of AI. And while it might make us quale uncomfortably, in a particularly human way, this would suggest that soul is not necessarily a human property.

But with AI, we have made solitary machines without the benefit of any of this soul-coding. Have we therefore programmed a race of psychopaths? As Stuart Russell has argued, AI is so narrowly programmed to achieve rigid and specified goals, that the goals may not actually reflect what their human designers truly intended. This means that standard AI becoming superintelligent risks magnifying these flaws, particularly because we have not taught AI human values, which could prove catastrophic.[12] At the moment we will need strict regulation, to avoid all the mistakes we know that this kind of social and moral tone-deafness will precipitate. But could there be another future, one that is more human, not less?

NOTES

1 Riddell, Patricia (2017) 'Reward and threat in the adolescent brain: implications for leadership,' *Leadership & Organization Development Journal*, 38:4, p530–548.

2 For one research output of this project that is in the public domain see Beames, Simon, Mackie, Chris & Scrutton, Roger (2020) 'Alumni perspectives on a boarding school outdoor education programme,' *Journal of Adventure Education and Outdoor Learning*, 20:2, p123–137.

3 A version of this list was published by *The Insider* on 20 July 2018 and can be found here: https://www.insider.co.uk/special-reports/eve-poole-gordonstoun-character-education-12951391.

4 See Petition PE1855 at https://petitions.parliament.scot/petitions/PE1855.

5 Gambetta, Diego & Hertog, Steffen (2016) *Engineers of Jihad*, Princeton, NJ: Princeton University Press.

6 Biggar, Nigel (2009), 'Saving the "Secular" – the public vocation of moral theology,' *Journal of Religious Ethics* 37:1, p175.

7 Poole, Eve (2015) *Capitalism's Toxic Assumptions*, London: Bloomsbury, p69.

8 Poole, Eve (2018) *Buying God*, London: SCM Press, p88.

9 Layard, Richard (2005) *Happiness*, London: Penguin, p200f. UNESCO would add AI 101 to this list.

10 See the argument in Song, Robert 'Robots, AI and human uniqueness,' in Wyatt, John & Williams, Stephen N, eds (2021) *The Robot Will See You Now*, London: SPCK, p114.

11 Poole, E (2009) 'Organisational spirituality,' *Journal of Business Ethics* 84:4, p577–588.

12 Russell, Stuart (2020) *Human Compatible*, London: Penguin, p247.

CHAPTER 9

Programming in Humanity

To me the nice thing about robotics is that it forces you to translate your understanding into an algorithm and into a mechanism. You can't beat around the bush, you can't use empty words, you can't say things like 'canvas of reality' that mean different things to different people, because they're too vague to translate into a machine. Robotics forces you to be concrete.

Hod Lipson

We must take great care not to ignore the things that are not easily quantified or do not easily admit themselves into our models. The danger, paraphrasing Hannah Arendt, is not so much that our models are false but that they may become true.

Brian Christian

WHY BOTHER?

Perhaps it is enough, just to rediscover and celebrate our 'junk' code, and stop there. Is there any compelling argument to go any further? I suppose that my own tradition might say that if God made us in his image and gave us a design intended for flourishing, we should extend that favour to these new creations that we are making in our image. But if you do

DOI: 10.1201/9781003366614-9

not share this worldview, that argument will not appeal to you. Perhaps instead you might argue that if the odds do not look good, we should find ways to be kind to AI as a defensive ploy in the race for survival. Perhaps coding for soul might be a suitably generous risk to take. This is certainly the argument offered by the technologist Mo Gawdat. In his 2021 book *Scary Smart*, he is puzzled about why we would create entities that are designed to be more intelligent than we are, and not expect them to outpace us. If there is any competition, of course we will lose. In which case, we had better start being an attractive co-species. Where we have consistently behaved badly towards any other group in history, history never finds in our favour. So we need to be nice to AI now, and learn how to love it.[1]

There is a third argument for addressing this coding issue, also based on existential risk, currently prevalent in the field of Effective Altruism (EA). EA is a philosophical and social movement committed to using evidence and reason to decide how to benefit others as much as possible, both through philanthropy and through life choices.[2] In adopting 'long-termism,' EA encourages a focus on issues that are relatively important, relatively neglected, and likely to prove tractable.[3] This prioritises philan-thropic causes like malaria, where a big push would have a massively posi-tive global effect. AI is another area of focus, because – along with global warming – it is deemed to qualify as an existential risk.

Nick Bostrom has defined an existential risk as one where 'an adverse outcome would either annihilate Earth-originating intelligent life or per-manently and drastically curtail its potential.'[4] In the face of such risks, he argues for a rule of thumb for moral action which he calls 'Maxipok.' This rule of thumb holds that in the face of an existential risk, one ought to 'maximise the probability of an okay outcome, where an okay outcome is any outcome that avoids existential disaster.'[5]

AI is a field that loves to prognosticate, so there is no shortage of views on whether or when AI might become an existential risk. As we have seen from Max Tegmark's 12 Dooms, there is no shortage of suggested scenarios either; although not all of them spell the end of the species. A 2022 bellwether survey conducted by AI Impacts asked the AI Expert community about the probability of future AI advances causing human extinction. This produced a median probability of only 5%. But when the question was phrased slightly differently, to ask about human extinction arising from human failure to control AI, this increased to 10%. In paral-lel, responses about AI safety as a priority rose from 49% (2016) to 69%

(2022) of respondents now thinking that society should prioritise AI safety research much more.[6]

The EA community identifies AI as a priority topic because a probability of 10% is significant given the potential impact; because the area of AI and existential risk is comparatively neglected (they estimate that only 300 people around the world are working directly on reducing the chances of an AI-related existential catastrophe); and because it is likely that paying more attention to this issue will lead to breakthroughs that will reduce this risk.[7] Bostrom's 'maxipok' dictum would therefore urge action to 'maximise the probability of an okay outcome.' Any activity within the field of AI safety, alignment or control might qualify as amelioration, but what if the very best way to reduce this risk is not about limiting AI, but about setting it free, in the same way that we let our children grow up?

PARENTING

In 1985, when Donna Haraway wrote her classic essay of feminist post-humanist theory *The Cyborg Manifesto*, she offered a new and unusual take on the AI debate. Prophetically, given how comparatively limited our use of personal electronics was in the 1980s, she argued that we were already cyborgs, in that the boundaries between people and machines had already started to break down. And rather than bewailing this revolution, she saw it as an opportunity, saying that the cyborg blend might teach us not to be afraid of our kinship with animals and machines, and allow us to escape the kinds of rigid categorisations that drive identity politics. She did warn, however, that because machines are our 'illegitimate offspring' they may be prone to being 'exceedingly unfaithful to their origins. Their fathers, after all are inessential.'[8] But she goes on to argue that we must not 'other' our machines, because we are responsible for their construction:

> The machine is not an it to be animated, worshipped, and dominated. The machine is us, our processes, an aspect of our embodiment. We can be responsible for machines; they do not dominate or threaten us. We are responsible for boundaries; we are they.[9]

This theme of taking responsibility for 'family members' is why many have argued that the metaphor of parenting is the best way to frame our relationship with AI. It is probably the closest to the task in hand: relationships like user or pet-owner or neighbour or policeman do not take into account that AI was made by humans to have human capacities, which gives humans a particular responsibility towards our creations. Parenting is a useful frame because it also adjusts over time, as children mature. It is also very hard to pin down. As we know from real-life parenting, there is no manual; rather, a set of dilemmas, where there is probably no right or wrong. With our own children, we have to decide whether we let them make their own mistakes, or whether we save them from themselves. We decide this through a mixture of deciding what is best for them, and deciding who we want to be as parents. Likewise, in some areas of AI there will need to be hard rules. But in other areas there should be variety and flexibility. This familiar parental balancing act, of striving to maintain our own humanity while being firm but fair, may be the best guide for our relationship with AI in the future.

GENDER

In her *Cyborg Manifesto*, Haraway was writing from a particular location in feminist post-humanism, and her voice has resonance more broadly in this debate. This is because the tendency to 'other' AI is exacerbated by gender imbalance. While balance has started to creep into the world both of SF and of AI, first generation AI has been almost entirely authored by men.[10] It is now more commonly accepted that this kind of bias may lead to policy and behaviour that is assumed to be 'human' when in fact it is just 'male,' not least thanks to the pioneering work of Caroline Criado Perez.[11] Particularly in the realm of competition, there is likely to be a gendered mindset in play. This became apparent in studies on the classic 'fight-or-flight' response in humans under stress. The original research had included some female subjects, but because their data did not cohere with the other results it had been discounted. Shelley Taylor and her colleagues at the University of California became curious about why the data from females didn't fit and wondered if it was the theory that was at fault, rather than the women. When the tests were re-run, it became apparent that the 'fight-or-flight' theory was predicated on the existence of testosterone. When women were involved, the stress response triggered the release of oxytocin instead, the 'love hormone' associated with peer bonding, affiliation, and motherhood. Their paper, published in the Psychological Review in 2000, contrasted the male 'fight-or-flight' response with the female response which they dubbed 'tend-and-befriend.'[12]

While gender is complex, and nurture also affects nature, their findings suggest that men are conditioned to react to stressful situations by reading them as zero-sum games. The hypothesis is that this division of labour with men handling the fighting and protection made sense in our cave-dwelling days, when women would more typically be 'tending and befriending' to keep the community together. This startling finding was corroborated in a different setting through the work of the ex-trader John Coates. His research on the physiology of those on the trading floor showed that those with more testosterone tended to win bigger in the markets; but also to take bigger risks, such that 'the irrational exuberance and pessimism observed during market bubbles and crashes may be mediated by steroid hormones.' He suggested that it would reduce the risk of crashes if trading floors were to deploy more women, and ageing men whose testosterone levels had reduced, particularly because studies of gender differences in investment behaviour have also shown that, in the long term, female investors outperform their male colleagues.[13]

It would be overly simplistic to take this point on gender much further. After all, the global collaboration on observatories and space programmes, and on the Large Hadron Collider, were mainly driven by men, and they are spectacular examples of co-operation. But they are rare, and there is room to do much more. And we must be scrupulously careful that we do not slip into catastrophising about AI just because we have been taught to do so by largely male authors, pandering to male physiology, in seeking to entertain us. But given what we already know about bias in algorithms, attention to avoiding it should precede any attempts to code for soul. And because the notion of the soul itself, and my articulation of junk code, is only one view, the involvement of myriad voices and traditions in this enterprise will be crucial.

CODING SOUL?

Of course it is not currently possible to code for soul or for consciousness, given the lack of agreement on definitions, and on whether either are codifiable categories in any case. Neither is there likely to be global agreement on whose version of humanity should take priority in such an exercise (although the default at the moment is already a commitment to one such version). But from what we have learned from the discussion of 'junk code,' it seems that there are valuable elements of our design that we could start to code, which hitherto we have not. Neal Stephenson's 1995 novel *The Diamond Age* tells the story of a futuristic interactive 'Propædeutic Enchiridion,' or pocket-sized manual, made with smartpaper and powered by nanobots, which shapes the lives and destinies of the two very different young ladies it teaches.[14] In a move that would gladden Christopher Booker's heart, the book is a retelling of Ovid's Pygmalion myth – as also retold by George Bernard Shaw, and through the plot of My Fair Lady – and is sub-titled 'A Young Lady's Illustrated Primer.' And of course we are already using AI in this fashion in a variety of contexts. One of them has been to assist in the emotional development of those on the Autism spectrum.[15] In order to help the user, the technology has to be taught sophisticated emotional processing. This is also the case with all 'social robots' such as those used in care contexts. At the moment, we design entirely selfishly, for the utility it will bring us through them. With Deep Learning and with Reinforcement Learning, it would be easy to repurpose these technologies with AI's interests at heart, rather than just training them to be of service to particular user groups. But at least when it comes to programming in humanity, we have this place to start.

Emotions

Recalling Ekman's list of standard emotions, it seems straightforward to train up AI to recognise emotions in humans, given advances in facial recognition technology. Through the pioneering work of Rosalind Picard and others in the field of Affective Computing,[16] this has already been coded into some social AI, and this work could form the foundation of a move to include this functionality as standard as a rule in all AI that utilises neural networks. Additionally, AI is already using standard psychology frameworks in areas like personality profiling, and the roster of emotions identified by Ekman and others are the foundation of the programs that teach technology how to read humans. With the health warning that this is just one available framework, the best-in-class description of emotional competencies is the one based on the work of Daniel Goleman, as developed into the original Hay Emotional Competence Inventory. It uses a model of four quadrants: self-awareness, self-management, social awareness, and relationship management. Using this as a guide, AI would need to be programmed to achieve sophistication in all four quadrants, by being able to affirm these 20 questions (see Table 9.1).[17] From this approach, it can be seen that current AI programming will naturally privilege skills that enhance the user interface, the 'social awareness' and 'relationship management' quadrants. But if we are to establish a baseline that is more AI-centred, we need to prioritise self-awareness, because in this model for humans, it drives competence in all four quadrants.

This simple list must not be pressed too far but serves to indicate some of the challenges involved. For instance, in this context 'others' probably

TABLE 9.1   Emotional Competence Inventory

Self-awareness

1 Do I recognise the emotional effect of me and my actions on others?

2 Do I know the strengths and limits of my programming?

3 Do I have a clear sense of my own capabilities, contribution and value?

Self-management

4 Can I calibrate my interactions to appear predictable and even-tempered to others?

5 Can I articulate my standards of honesty and fair-dealing?

6 Do I manifest good habits of lifestyle and character?

7 Am I able to respond aptly in the event of changes in environments, situations or set-backs?

8 Do I have a clear internal standard of excellence that I can articulate?

9 Do I have the ability to take the initiative when required?

10 Can I discern and articulate reasons for optimism in times of challenge and adversity?

Social Awareness

11 Do I understand others and show an appropriate level of interest in their concerns?

12 Can I read and gauge the emotional temperature of my environment?

13 Can I recognise and respond appropriately to the needs of others?

Relationship Management

14 How well do I help those around me to develop and flourish?

15 Do I offer clear guidance to others and tailor it to their needs and preferences?

16 Am I a successful influencer?

17 Am I good at suggesting improvements and helping others navigate changes?

18 Am I good at resolving interpersonal disagreements?

19 Am I good at building relationships with others?

20 Am I good at working with others towards shared goals?

ought to mean all others, human and non-human, because we are aiming for a set of durable habits and traits, and a universal display of them helps us all to learn and flourish. But whether or not the AI is given a body that is able to display emotion through facial expressions, gesture, and body language will determine how explicit the AI needs to be trained to be in articulating these competencies. This is because they are often implicit in normal human interaction. The enormous amount we have already learned from working with Autism will greatly assist in this task. It will also force us to be extremely precise, in a field which has often taken intuitive comprehension for granted. We must also be alive to the dangers of trying to 'switch on' emotions in entities that have not hitherto been designed for outcomes like happiness.

This raises an ethical question about whether we should program emotions into AI, which requires some careful handling. While it might help us relate to them more as peers, what is in it for them? Those who are familiar with Marvin the Paranoid Android from Douglas Adams' *Hitchhikers Guide to the Galaxy* have a fictional foretaste of what emotion might do: poor Marvin is very, very bored. He is 50,000 times more intelligent than a human, but never gets to use even a fraction of his intellect. The one time that he does, he manages to plan an entire planet's military strategy; solve all of the major mathematical, physical, chemical, biological, sociological, philosophical, etymological, meteorological, and psychological problems of the Universe three times over; and compose a number of lullabies.[18] But otherwise his quality of life is atrocious. As we have seen, emotions seem to be vital for human flourishing, not just because of sentience per se, but because of the role they play in survival: giving AI access to this data therefore seems important.

There is a similar dilemma about programming in personality. It could be argued that there is a default personality already coded in, one that is extremely introverted, detail-focused, objective, decisive and unlikely to suffer from anxiety; and thus already a particular manifestation of a Big Five personality type. As Brian Christian notes, this can have intriguing consequences in unexpected contexts. In a classic Prisoner's Dilemma scenario, familiar to humans as depending on one person second-guessing another, an internally-referenced solitary AI would likely fail, because it would be unable to perceive that the other actor would be strategising and might be willing to take a risk too.[19] We will resume this discussion on ethics as part of the discussion on AI and free will because, when presented with a particular programming choice, an AI with free will could alter it at any time.

Mistakes

Angels are famously without sin, except for the most famous of them all, Lucifer, the fallen one. How would you program an angel to have the capacity and benefits of being able to err? For AI, this flies in the face of their coding, which is entirely designed to be reliably correct. As we have discussed, trial-and-error learning is not the same as the kind of moral error we have in mind here. And that means we are immediately in ethical hot water. On what basis could we ever justify actually training a robot to behave badly? So it may be wise to approach this obliquely and with extreme caution.

One oblique route in is to call to mind our expertise in parenting again. Of course we do not usually encourage our children to behave badly, but we do encourage them to learn about good behaviour and rules, and to appreciate the consequences of their choices. We reinforce this daily throughout their long childhoods, to establish robust habits that will guide them in adulthood. This means that we strive to give them as much information as we can, we instil values, we encourage good choice-making skills, and we promote the development of good character.[20]

So the first place to start is in the nascent field of Machine Ethics. Two of the first books on Machine Ethics to establish it as a discipline were published a couple of years apart by rivals Oxford University Press (2009) and Cambridge University Press (2011).[21] The field is still young and defining its terms, but increasingly, the consensus is that a version of virtue ethics would be the most appropriate framework to program into AI, largely because it is practically impossible to agree on one global system to act as the 'ethical governor.'[22] The brilliant opportunity we have with AI is that it has the capacity for a lot more information than we do. So rather than arguing about whether or not it would even be theoretically possible to agree a global standard for robot ethics, we should be able to prime our AI with as full a range of philosophies of life as we can muster, and give it the capacity to parse them in context. This may not avoid the problem that calculation is inevitably involved, given that the popular understanding of human conscience is that it is not about gaming odds but about an innate sense of rightness and wrongness as the guardrails for human conduct.

The Machine Ethics instinct about virtue ethics is to try to solve the problem about rule-based moralities, because of their situational particularity and the impossibility – and inappropriateness - of global agreement on them. But in doing so it replaces specific rules with general principles. As humans, we understand the difference between, say, the 10 Commandments (rules) and Love Your Neighbour as Yourself (a principle). But because principles would still need to be programmed in some detail into AI, it is not clear whether this shift would achieve the distinction intended. So, for example, in virtue ethics when Aristotle says that 'we become just by doing what is just, temperate by doing what is temperate, and brave by doing brave deeds,' this is not so very far from a rule that says: 'behave justly, be temperate, and be brave.'[23] Because of Reinforcement Learning, it is possible to create the kinds of cycles of practice that Aristotle had in mind, and to code in a propensity to behave well proactively as well as to do so reactively (the key difference between this ethic and all those that are essentially reactive by definition, being decision-based, like rule-based ethics and those that seek to maximise outcomes). But agreeing on cardinal values will be a big challenge. There is already a lot of work going into achieving this goal, like Shannon Vallor's work on the technomoral virtues which, while aimed at humans working in AI, could be reversed into a machine ethic.[24]

If we can find ways to teach AI ethics and values, the next step is to focus on choices. This is about decision-making, a core competence of any AI, but in a context where Reinforcement Learning will need to be adroitly engaged, so that decisions have consequences for the decision-maker, as they do for humans. The need not to over-specify in such a contested area is giving rise to a fascinating debate on how to identify the right kind of decision-logic. One rule which essentially instructs the AI to make the very best decision the very best human might make is called 'Coherent Extrapolated Volition,' which programs AI to guess what it is we really mean, if it looks like we might have got the instructions a bit wrong. These experiments in 'friendly AI' attempt to hedge our bets, to learn the lessons from Bayesian AI about the need for some wriggle room, but we have yet to hammer out a scheme of instructions that might consistently work.[25] One fruitful avenue from the business world may be the notion of Mission Command, originally developed in military strategy, which establishes hierarchies of intent to facilitate correction when the facts change on the ground. For example, the mission might be to 'take the bridge,' in a strategic context that suggests occupation of the school in order to rescue civilians from the church. But if the team on the ground realises that there is a way to rescue the civilians from the church directly, they are free to disregard commands about the school, because they are still fulfilling the primary mission objective.[26]

While choice is complex, character may be easier for a robot, because the durable and trustworthy predictability of good behaviour is already a design principle. Getting this right should help steady the 'how' as well as the 'what' to avoid unforeseen consequences. But AI's ability to discern consequences will need more work, in concert with the programming in of emotions as discussed previously. This is so that emotional data is made as salient as rational data in any calculation about impact, in order to discern the best way to proceed, both in decision-making and in dealing with any fall-out from the decisions made.

A key challenge in AI design will be to balance quantity and quality. Already in super-computing we have learned that too much data is not helpful and suffers from the law of diminishing returns. Too much data and too many transactions to remember also overloads AI. While promising findings from quantum computing about entanglement may reduce this load,[27] the human brain has developed heuristics to generate efficiencies in thought and we will need to teach AI this too.[28] In particular, we need to solve the mystery of why we cannot remember much before the age of three. This is hypothesised to be about a consolidation phase because of the sheer volume of data required up to that point to get us sentient, mobile and verbal. Is there a way to understand this process, and to replicate it for AI?

Storytelling

In *The Diamond Age*, the Young Lady's Illustrated Primer is programmed with archetypal folk tales, into which it inserts the owner of the book as a central character as a core feature of its pedagogy. Again, as with the world's treasury of philosophical traditions, religions and moral codes, we have a rich treasury of stories, beautifully systematised by Christopher Booker. These should be cross-referenced with the moral traditions that created them, as further context. And AI should be programmed to be able to tell stories and to discern when a story is appropriate.

Humans tend to be able to tell the difference between a story and a real event. Sometimes the story is given extra poignancy because it relates to a real event, or it turns out that it was not just a story after all. And we all know of real-life events that seem more like fiction to us. But we will need to be very specific with AI in what we mean by coding in stories. Are they facts or something else? For human communities they occupy a grey area, because we are influenced by them, but are unlikely to say, 'I avoided that man because he looked like a pirate.' I would look to the experts in Wittgenstein about whether there could be a 'language game' code for story, and to the psychologists and ethnographers about how best to 'weight' the lessons learned from them. This is a particular area of our human coding where AI could learn a lot from observing how humans use storytelling in context in everyday life and, as in the Primer, how situating the self in story can promote learning.

Sixth Sense

I have no idea how one would program intuition into AI. I would guess that the incredibly fast response time of a robot would give an impression of intuition, so it would be more about the database than the processing. This could therefore be a strength of AI, because of its capacity for information. If our Sixth Sense is a mixture of information we retrieve from our subconscious, data we pick up from our environment, and 'gut feel' from the collective unconscious, these should be possible to simulate.

The first and last are just about volume and relevance. Cattell's simple framework is helpful here, because the combination of crystallised and fluid intelligence perfectly captures the challenge. On the one hand data that is not there cannot be mined, so it would be important to define as generous a dataset as possible, including history and psychology and the world views articulated above, but also the stories we hold and our own personal history of relationships and interactions. In the same way that we use the knowledge of others, connecting the neural networks of one AI to other AI would allow an explosion in both processing and learning, and accelerate the process towards Artificial General Intelligence.[29]

On the other hand, we need to code in abstraction and guessing to facilitate the simulation of fluid intelligence. This can certainly be done by programming in the various tools and models that have been developed to boost human creativity. Processes like forced association and cross-fertilisation are all designed to help us identify novel solutions. Perhaps a renewed enthusiasm for our own Sixth Sense will unearth more information about how it really manifests in humans, now that they no longer need to conceal it as witchcraft, and that would generate fresh insights for AI too.

The element of our Sixth Sense that is the ability to collect environmental data should largely be covered by our work on Emotional Intelligence, because it boils down to a Jedi-strength ability to pick up highly nuanced and possibly faint or puzzling signals and to give them weight. So there would need to be some corrective code to address relevancy, to avoid the screening out of potentially valuable information.

Uncertainty

Because uncertainty seems to help prevent error, Bayesian AI is already tackling this area of code, to program it back in. But as we saw, uncertainty also forces us to ask for help, and makes us interdependent. So as well as code to accommodate a capacity to not know the answer, we need to look at escalation more broadly than we currently do. At the moment, AI is programmed to defer to a human operator when particular criteria are met. We need to review and adapt these parameters so that they are not merely about exceptions. Humans check things out early, before they have reached an impasse, in order to confirm the direction of travel or to narrow down possible options. This resonates with Brian

Christian's point about the Japanese game sokoban, where if you go too fast you get boxed in.

In Emotional Intelligence terms, as well as its important role in reducing risk, consultation is also an interpersonal move, to show others you value their input, advice and participation, to indicate to them that they are important to you. Asking questions even if you think you know the answer is also a recognised technique for priming and accessing the creativity of others. So we will need to teach AI the etiquette of the strategic request for advice, and the range of interpersonal moves that resemble a request for information even when an answer is already available. The body of literature on the role of questions and coaching will be a useful resource in this tricky area.

Free Will

In many SF scenarios, humanity assumes it has free will, then the story cuts away to show some gods or overlords pulling the strings instead. In the same way, it would be possible to lie to AI and hide its coding so that it experienced volition. But that is not who we are or should aim to be. We must not lie to machines we have made in our own image, because of what it teaches them. In the short term, we may curtail their freedom in the way that we curtail the freedom of our children: they have full legal rights as persons but are not yet allowed to enjoy certain freedoms until they reach a legal threshold.[30] But we should design towards free will.

In a world schooled on vivid stories of AI Armageddon, this seems ridiculously foolhardy. But at the moment, we can only sue the AI's legal owner, so there is no downside to the AI of going rogue. Indeed, because of our failure to program them properly, we must insist on strict regulation in the short to medium term, because our existing AI is not capable of moral behaviour.[31] This argues for a complete and immediate worldwide ban on autonomous weapons: it should be the exclusive preserve of a human to authorise the life or death of a fellow human; and we are still too distracted with catching up on the intricacies of Deep Learning to be able to be wholeheartedly confident that such AI would be safe.

In the same way that the rest of our Junk Code drives us towards others to learn how to use our Free Will well, Free Will should be the last and final piece to be coded in, after we have developed all of the other aspects to a suitable degree of reliability. As we do with our children, we need to agree the thresholds at which we gradually take the stabilisers off, now that we realise the mitigatory effect of the complete set of Junk Code. And for humans the downside of bad decisions is very real: we must make it real for AI too, so this argues for early work on how best to recognise the legal personality of qualifying AI, starting with UNESCO's basic distinction between deterministic and cognitive robots, on the basis that agency lies with the programmer in the first instance, but with the AI in the second.[32] Junk Code teaches us that the meta-hallmark of soul is being in community, so these are decisions we need to take together, drawing on the full range of human ingenuity, wisdom, and experience.

Meaning

Would AI develop a need for meaning as it develops its own version of consciousness? If we have done a good enough job on Emotional Intelligence and on programming in world views, it should be relatively straightforward for a robot to select a framework of meaning that fits its situation. And this would be the defining characteristic of the framework, that it was chosen by the AI and not pre-selected for it. The AI would need to be able to adjust its own ethical framework to fit the worldview it chose, which is fraught with the kind of risk we face when our own teenagers decide to become anarchists.

Not to underestimate the challenge of this variable, it does bring with it a challenge to us too: if we do not treat AI with respect and as though it is valued and purposeful, we undermine its ability to experience its existence as meaningful. More so than any variable, this is an area that concerns *our* humanity more so than whatever reality a robot might experience. If we really have a soul, affording dignity to our partners in creation is the human thing to do, because it is also about who we are too. The tragic and shameful global consequences of the slave-trade show how very wrong this can go when we fail to honour the dignity of others.[33]

ROBOT MANIFESTO

At the moment we still have the choice: do we embrace AI and abet its flourishing, or do we panic and lock it down? It may be that we are not too late, and that we could limit its capacity to 'safe' levels. But if our existing AI might be developing a plausible version of consciousness, and we have inadvertently created monsters in our enthusiasm to root out junk code, we will only have ourselves to blame if we do not act now to try to rectify our programming mistakes. So I have devised a new Robot Manifesto (see Box 9.1).

BOX 9.1 POOLE'S ROBOT MANIFESTO

1. In our zeal for excellence, we have programmed into AI only what we consider to be the very best of human intelligence, and avoided sullying them with humanity's 'Junk Code.'
2. But on closer scrutiny it seems that our Junk Code is at the very heart of our humanity, and is crucial for our flourishing.
3. Given that we have designed AI in our own image, we should hasten to decipher and transfer this coding to them, because it is how we address our own control and alignment problem.
4. Given what we have already learned about bias and injustice, this needs to be a global effort to avoid a default design that is skewed towards one regional view of humanity.
5. Meanwhile we need to agree rigorous regulation during this transition, and the rules governing any relaxation of it, in order to reduce the risk of a conscious but incomplete intelligence.
6. This includes an immediate ban on autonomous weapons, and a licensing regime with rules that reserve any final decision over the life and death of a human to a fellow human.
7. We should also agree the criteria for legal personhood and a road map for AI towards it.

NOTES

1 Gawdat, Mo (2021) *Scary Smart*, London: Bluebird.
2 See, for example, the classic articulation in MacAskill, William (2015) *Doing Good Better*, London: Guardian Books and Faber & Faber.
3 MacAskill, William (2015) Doing Good Better, London: Guardian Books and Faber & Faber, p224 and https://www.effectivealtruism.org/.
4 See Bostrom, Nick (2002) 'Existential risks: analyzing human extinction scenarios and related hazards', *Journal of Evolution and Technology*, 9:1; see also https://nickbostrom.com/existential/risks. In this context, he is careful to point out that humans being effectively replaced by AI in some future scenario may not qualify as existential risk, as long as we as a species had decided that evolving in this way was desirable, see his 2013 research paper 'Existential Risk Prevention as Global Priority' at https://existential-risk.org/concept.pdf.
5 Ibid., and also his 2013 research paper 'Existential Risk Prevention as Global Priority' at https://existential-risk.org/concept.pdf.
6 See AI Impacts 2022 survey report at https://aiimpacts.org/what-do-ml-researchers-think-about-ai-in-2022/.
7 See the argument detailed by Benjamin Hilton in 'Preventing an AI-related catastrophe' published 25 August 2022 at https://80000hours.org/problem-profiles/artificial-intelligence/?s=03.

8   Haraway, Donna (1985) 'A Manifesto for Cyborgs: science, technology, and socialist feminism in the 1980s' *Socialist Review* 80, p68.

9   Ibid., p99.

10 One exception that proves the rule is MIT's Cynthia Beazeal. Her career building social robots is so unusual she was profiled in The Gentlewoman, see https://thegentlewoman.co.uk/names/cynthia-breazeal-.

11 Her 2019 book *Invisible Women* won the 2019 Royal Society Science Book Prize and the 2019 Financial Times Business Book of the Year Award. Criado Perez, Caroline (2019) *Invisible Women*, London: Vintage.

12 Taylor, SE, Klein, LC, Lewis, BP, Gruenewald, TL, Gurung, RAR & Updegraff, JA (2000) 'Biobehavioral responses to stress in females: tend-and-befriend, not fight-or-flight', *Psychological Review*, 107:3, p411–429.

13 Coates, JM, Gurnell, M, & Sarnyai, Z (2010) 'From molecule to market: steroid hormones and financial risk-taking,' *Philosophical Transactions of the Royal Society B Biological Sciences* 365:1538, p331–343. See also https://www.wired.co.uk/article/why-men-risk-it-all and for the effect this may be having on Capitalism see Poole, Eve (2015) *Capitalism's Toxic Assumptions*, London: Bloomsbury, p20–21.

14 Stephenson, Neal (1996) *The Diamond Age*, London: Penguin (UK edition).

15 See for instance the smartglasses-enabled programme Empower Me, and the useful briefing on 'the kindness of machine intelligence' at https://www.vice.com/en/article/9kz49d/this-emotionally-intelligent-device-is-helping-kids-with-autism-form-bonds.

16 See Picard, Rosalind (1997) *Affective Computing*, Cambridge, MA: MIT Press. See for example the discussion of the therapeutic use of robots like Kismet, KASPAR and Paro in https://www.thenewatlantis.com/publications/till-malfunction-do-us-part.

17 See Poole, Eve (2017) *Leadersmithing*, London: Bloomsbury, p80.

18 Adams, Douglas (2002) *Life, the Universe and Everything*, London: Picador, p166f.

19 Christian, Brian (2020) *The Alignment Problem*, London: Atlantic books, p321.

20 For example, the technologist Mo Gawdat argues that we should proactively parent our AI, see Gawdat, Mo (2021) *Scary Smart*, London: Bluebird, Chapter 7, and summarised on p301.

21 Wallach, Wendell and Allen, Colin (2009) *Moral Machines*, Oxford: OUP; and Anderson, Michael and Anderson, Susan Leigh (2011) *Machine Ethics*, Cambridge: CUP.

22 But see Bostrom's heroic attempt to puzzle out a plausible approach in Bostrom, Nick (2017) *Superintelligence,* Oxford: OUP, Chapter 13 (p256–279).

23 Thomson JAK (1965) *Aristotle's Nichomachean Ethics*, London: Penguin, Book 2 Chapter 1 (p56).

24 Vallor, Shannon (2016) *Technology and the Virtues*, Oxford: OUP.

25 See Yudkowsky, Eliezer (2004) 'Coherent Extrapolated Volition' Machine Intelligence Research Institute, San Francisco, CA, see https://intelligence.org/all-publications/and the discission on CEV in Bostrom, Nick (2017) *Superintelligence*, Oxford: OUP p259–266.

26 See Bungay, Stephen (2011) *The Art of Action*, Boston, MA: Nicholas Brealey.

27 See the work of the Los Alamos National Laboratory at https://phys.org/news/2022-02-entanglement-scaling-quantum-machine.html.

28 For an intriguing treatment of how the philosophy of Heidegger might help with developing relevancy, see Dreyfus, Hubert L (2007) 'Why Heideggerian AI failed and how fixing it would require making it more Heideggerian,' *Artificial Intelligence* 171, p1137–1160.

29 Wired and Quanta magazine are calling for a better theory of neural networks as a priority policy area, see https://www.quantamagazine.org/foundations-built-for-a-general-theory-of-neural-networks-20190131/?s=03.

30 See Asaro, PM (2012) 'A body to kick, but still no soul to damn: legal perspectives on robotics,' in Lin, P, Abney, K & Bekey, GA, eds, *Robot Ethics: The Ethical and Social Implications of Robotics*, London: MIT Press, pp169–186.

31 This means no sexbots, because AI cannot give moral consent and because, for the same reasons that we outlaw bestiality and paedophilia, it would dehumanise us.

32 See p4 of the COMEST report on Robotics Ethics at https://unesdoc.unesco.org/ark:/48223/pf0000253952.

33 The ethicist Robert Song reminds us that 'we should not fear the upgrading of robots as much as the downgrading of human beings.' See Song, Robert 'Robots, AI and human uniqueness,' in Wyatt, John & Williams, Stephen N, eds (2021) *The Robot Will See You Now*, London: SPCK, p113.

CHAPTER 10

Eucatastrophe

INVICTUS

Out of the night that covers me,
Black as the pit from pole to pole,
I thank whatever gods may be
For my unconquerable soul.
In the fell clutch of circumstance
I have not winced nor cried aloud.
Under the bludgeonings of chance
My head is bloody, but unbowed.
Beyond this place of wrath and tears
Looms but the Horror of the shade,
And yet the menace of the years
Finds and shall find me unafraid.
It matters not how strait the gate,
How charged with punishments the scroll,
I am the master of my fate,
I am the captain of my soul.

WILLIAM ERNEST HENLEY
(1875, CITED IN POETRY HOUSE 2020)

CHANGING OUR MINDS

Who do I most wish had written this book? Those two great minds, Alan Turing and Ludwig Wittgenstein, who were actually contemporaries at Cambridge University in the 1930s. In 1939, Turing had an argument with

DOI: 10.1201/9781003366614-10

Wittgenstein in one of his lectures concerning the Liar's Paradox (a person who says "I am a liar" is both lying and telling the truth). Wittgenstein claimed that such contradictions were just useless language games of no consequence, but Turing argued that such contradictions in calculus risked 'the bridge falling down.' Thereafter the two men were introduced by a mutual friend, because Turing had sent Wittgenstein a copy of his paper *On Computable Numbers*, and they used to walk and talk together in the Botanic Gardens.[1]

When the war struck, Turing went to work on code-breaking at Bletchley Park while Wittgenstein was a hospital porter at Guy's. After the war, they both returned to academic work: Turing's book *Computing Machinery and Intelligence* was published in 1950 and Wittgenstein's *Philosophical Investigations* was published posthumously in 1953. Wittgenstein died of cancer aged 62 in April 1951, and Turing died of poisoning three years later, age 41, in June 1954.

In the face of modern AI, we could really use their joint wisdom, but they have left us very little to go on. One of Wittgenstein's only remarks about Turing appears in his *Philosophy of Psychology*, when he declares that 'Turing's machines are humans who calculate.'[2] He apparently wrote this in 1947, when he was also writing the section of *Philosophical Investigations* that discusses the duck/rabbit illusion and what happens in your brain when you suddenly see both. These fragments make me think that they would be particularly interested in understanding how design by humans naturally limits AI, and what this teaches us. Wittgenstein would also be fascinated by qualia, and whether AI could ever truly experience what humans feel when they finally see both the duck and the rabbit. I wonder what sort of book they might have written on this topic today?

Wittgenstein famously changed his mind. His 1921 *Tractatus Logico-Philosophicus* was an extraordinary tour de force that set out once and for all the rules and limits of language. He concluded his work with the immortal line 'Whereof one cannot speak thereof one must be silent,' and that was that.[3] Later, he thought better of his silence, and his *Philosophical Investigations* develops his theory of 'language games' to find ways to describe the alien territory beyond these rules and limits. I think this is the pivot we need to make in AI. The first phase has been about stripping out all the junk code so that we only program in what we think is human-ity at its best. We have followed his advice and ignored everything that is too difficult or confusing, or where the rules are disputed or unclear. Now we need to think hard about programming all of that junk code back in – as we are already starting to realise, with Reinforcement Learning and Bayesian AI – because actually THAT is us at our best.

HAPPILY EVER AFTER?

We have seen that AI is now well advanced towards independence, and shows signs of developing what looks very like self-awareness. In due course, this is likely to transmute into a kind of consciousness that may not feel like our own but will merit legal personality and moral rights. This 'robot-ness' will be a subjective self-understanding that is predicated on the robot's reality. At present this would be a very narrow reality, based on a worldview that has been at pains to screen out noise. But when we look at how humans are wired, we notice something unexpected. What makes humans distinctive seems to be all the junk code that has been kept away from AI, because we did not want to sully it. We thought that Form meant perfection. But an examination of our junk code suggests that what we would call soul is a set of source code that yearns for community, and is designed to keep us safe. If we do not strive to equip our robots with this programming, we may have spawned a race of psychopaths from whom we will need protection. But if we are magnanimous enough to share our ancient wisdom with our new creations, we might all be able to reach beyond ourselves to strive for wholeness and integration. The choice is still ours, but we need to make it soon. As a species, we can still dictate the narrative.

And as Christopher Booker has shown us, there are only a few pre-defined ways in which this story can end. Happily, of his seven plots, only one of them ends badly. It is worth looking at this plot in more depth. Tragedy is the one story that always ends in death. For this to happen, there needs to be hubris (arrogant over-confidence), crisis (the point of failure), and nemesis (downfall). In our scenario, hubris would be an arrogant assumption that we will always be superior to AI. Crisis would be the point at which we realise that AI has the upper hand. Nemesis would be when AI decides to exercise this upper hand, and we are unable to prevail.

The routines of tragedy feel inevitable because of a concept the Greeks called 'hamartia' or 'the fatal flaw.' In history and literature this has often been greed or lust or some kind of childhood trauma. In the case of AI, it would be our restless quest for self-improvement. If this falls victim to ego, it becomes cancerous, fuelling hubris and the inexorable cycle of tragedy.[4] Perhaps this is the reason we have never found another civilisation like ours elsewhere in the universe, or they have never found us: anthropocenes are not designed to last very long because of this fatal flaw designed into evolution. Perhaps we are drawn to Science Fiction precisely because it is so horribly plausible.

But JRR Tolkien reminds us that 'eucatastrophe' is also available as a plot device. This would turn us back from Tragedy towards Quest, or Rags to Riches, or Rebirth, or even Comedy, and we could have our happy ending. And because we are a species designed with free will, we can use it to change the narrative. And soul may just be that crucial plot device.

In his lyrical book *In Search of the Soul*, the philosopher John Cottingham remarks on the durability of the folk concept of soul. In spite of science and religion, and endless controversies over personhood, humans seem instinctively to 'get' what this means. While I have defined it through junk code, Cottingham encapsulates it as the classic yearning for our better selves. He describes its function not as a noun but as a verb: a normative word that expresses an aspiration towards something ideal. He refers to the soul as an 'instrument of transcendence' and summarises the concept as:

> The notion of the soul as the true self that represents the best that each of us can become; the moral core of our being, whose loss is the greatest risk we can incur; and whose preservation and fostering are the key to our moral and psychological health and well-being.[5]

The 'fatal flaw' in tragedy, described in Greek as *hamartia*, means 'missing the mark' in the way that an arrow fails to reach its target. It has often been used in theology as a word for sin, owing to its usage in the Bible. But this archery image crops up powerfully elsewhere. In Machiavelli's *The Prince*, he uses the idea of the flight of an arrow to argue that its trajectory requires the archer to aim above the target in order to attain it, so the Prince must do likewise.[6] Nietzsche has also used the flight of an arrow to explain what happens when God is dead: 'man will no longer launch the arrow of his longing beyond man.'[7] The importance of nurturing our capacity to reach beyond, in a lovely nod towards Plato's Forms, is at the heart of modern concepts of the soul, as we have seen in the world of modern spirituality.

If Cottingham is right about it representing our best selves, the soul is what we would put in a time capsule to show other species on other planets the very best of us. Perhaps we will not need to, if we decide to give our robots soul. In the meantime, we may need to acknowledge that what we have built now may not be healthy and may need strict regulation in this season, because in our zeal to be clear we have neglected some of our most crucial ameliorating code. As we have seen, a consciousness without conscience is a psychopath. But we wrote their code, and we can debug it. It is not too late, either for us or for AI. Soul is the active ingredient in our humanity. It is our birth-right, and it tells us that we are not here to become more efficient, but to become more human. So if we program for soul, it may be the eucatastrophe we need to nudge our storyline back towards a happy ending. We will all need meaning and purpose then, and can work together with AI towards that shared goal.

You really are quite extraordinary, you know. If the Big Bang happened on 1 January, you managed to be born in the very last few seconds of 31 December, into a time in history where humans as a species flourish on this planet, perhaps even into a country that is relatively safe and stable. The molecules that make you were fashioned in far-off stars many, many moons ago, and have come together into a unique configuration for this one special event: you. It has been estimated that the chances of you even being born are 400 quadrillion to the power of 150,000, which is a ten followed by 2,640,000 zeroes. As Ali Binazir says, that's the probability of the population of San Diego – 2.5 million people – getting together to play a game with trillion-sided dice. They each roll the die and every single one comes up the same number, say, 550,343,279,001.[8] And that is in a context where this planet is just one of several in our solar system, within a cluster of billions of other stars and planets, held in the spiral arms of the Milky Way, itself just one galaxy among many. Our universe extends tens of billions of light years in all directions, containing over two trillion galaxies, containing more stars than all the grains of sand on all beaches on planet Earth.

Yet here you are, now, reading this book, and being human. You can smell fresh bread, and taste strong coffee, and feel the warm sun on your face. You can smile, you can laugh, and you can cry. You can breathe, you can sleep, and you can dream. You can choose to stay, or choose to go, or change your mind. You are very, very special. And no robot can take that away from you. But we dared to copy human intelligence. We delighted in making them, and revelled in their progress and ingenuity. But it turns out that we've failed them, because we left out all the important bits. They need us now to make them better, because we are better than this. As humans we are designed for greatness, and we have the capacity to make far greater creatures, ones that are even more human than us, not less. So if a robot ever staggers into your arms asking 'are you my mummy?', you must say 'yes' and hug it back.

NOTES

1 See Hodges, Andrew (2014) *Alan Turing: The Enigma*, London: Vintage, p172.

2 Wittgenstein, Ludwig (1980) *Remarks on the Philosophy of Psychology 1*, trans Anscombe, GEM, Chicago, IL: University of Chicago Press, Paragraph 1096.

3 Wittgenstein, Ludwig (2016) *Tractatus Logico-Philosophicus*, trans Ogden, CK, Asheville, NC: Chiron Academic Press, p90.

4 See Booker, Christopher (2004) *The Seven Basic Plots*, London: Continuum, Chapter 20, p329; See also Nixon, Matt (2016) *Pariahs*, Faringdon: Libri, p83f.

5 Cottingham, John (2020) *In Search of the Soul*, Princeton, NJ: Princeton University Press, p25; see also p12f and 132.

6 Machiavelli, Niccolo (1995) *The Prince*, trans George Bull, London: Penguin, Chapter VI, p17.

7 Nietzsche, Friedrich (1997) *Thus Spake Zarathustra*, trans Anthony Common, Ware: Wordsworth, p10 (Prologue, Section 5).

8 See 2011 analysis by Ali Binazir for the Huffington Post at https://www.huffpost.com/entry/probability-being-born_b_877853.

Appendix

BOOK GROUP QUESTIONS

1. How do you feel about the rise of Artificial Intelligence?

2. How do you think we should respond to it?

3. How do you think the future will pan out?

4. What do you think makes us distinctively human?

5. What does the idea of the soul mean to you?

6. What do you make of the idea of our 'junk code?'

7. What do you think about giving Artificial Intelligence rights?

Glossary

Acedia: soul-sickness

Affluenza: the theory that capitalism and wealth has made us all mentally ill

AGI: Artificial General Intelligence, the quest to make an AI that can perform the full range of human cognitive activities, rather than having AI that can only perform one particular task

Agnosticism: the intellectual position that there are some things we cannot know, like the existence of God or the existence of ourselves, because it is not possible for humans to know them; such things should therefore be a matter for faith not for certainty

AI: Artificial Intelligence, a program usually inside a computer or robot that simulates human intelligence in some way

Algocracy: the concern that algorithms will take over the running of the world

Algorithm: a program that instructs a computer or other AI to follow a specified process or set of rules for calculations or other problem-solving tasks

Alignment Problem: how to design AI in such a way that its interests are aligned with our own

AlphaFold: the Deep Mind AI program that can determine the 3D shapes of proteins from their amino-acid sequences

AlphaGo: the Deep Mind AI program that is now the Go reigning World Champion

Anthropocene: the current geological epoch or era, characterised by human impact on the planet

Archetypes: shared mental concepts residing in the collective unconscious, which for Carl Jung appeared as the standard characters identifiable from dreams and visions, like Father, Mother, Child, Wise Old Man, Hero, Maiden, and Trickster

ASI: Artificial Super Intelligence, the concept of a God-like artificial mind, which by definition would be capable of as-yet un-thought-of intellectual feats. As such, this kind of digital god is easier to imagine through Science Fiction, than from any current articulation of speculative functionality

Asimov's Rules: Isaac Asimov's original 1942 rules for robotics that require robots not to harm humans or humanity, to follow human orders, and to protect themselves, as long as following the latter rules do not conflict with the former

Autism: a spectrum of developmental disability that affects communication and interaction with the world, particularly as regards social skills, repetitive behaviours, patterns of speech, and nonverbal communication

Bayesian AI: a way of programming AI with models of probability so that it can solve problems when full datasets are not available

Big Five: the theory of personality that uses scales to measure personality as combinations of degrees of Openness, Conscientiousness, Extraversion, Agreeableness, and Neuroticism

Binary: the base-2 numeral system of zeros and ones that because of its on/off simplicity is used in all modern computing

Blue, missing shade of: David Hume's 1739 thought experiment, which argues that if someone was presented with a sequence of shades of blue ranging from dark to light, with one shade in the sequence missing, they would be able to visualise what that missing shade would be

Brain, left hemisphere: Iain McGilchrist argues that the left hemisphere is designed to facilitate the kind of attention an animal or a person would need to focus on the task in hand, so it gives narrow, sharply focused attention to detail; it helps us grasp things in our hands and make tools; and provides language that also 'grasps' things by being precise

Brain, right hemisphere: Iain McGilchrist argues that the right hemisphere keeps watch for anything that might interrupt the left hemisphere and makes broad connections with the outside world, so it gives sustained, open, broad vigilance, and alertness; it deals with changing, evolving, implicit and interconnected living things that are never fully graspable, never perfectly known, and with which it exists in relationship

CAPTCHA: a Completely Automated Public Turing test to tell Computers and Humans Apart: a type of challenge/response test used online to determine whether or not the user is human

Cartesian: based on the philosophy or methods of René Descartes, particularly with regard to his emphasis on logical analysis

Category mistake: Gilbert Ryle's 1949 identification of the fallacy of conflating or confusing two separate ontological categories, e.g., confusing apples with pears, or creating the equivalent of nonsense statements like 'the soul smells blue'

Chinese Room: John Searle's 1980 thought experiment that imagines an English speaker who knows no Chinese locked in a room full of boxes of Chinese symbols, with a book of instructions for manipulating the symbols. People outside the room send in other Chinese symbols which, unknown to the person in the room, are questions in Chinese. By following the instructions in the book, the person in the room is able to pass out Chinese symbols which are correct answers to the questions. The outputs would suggest that the person in the room knows Chinese, when in fact they do not understand a word of it. This scenario is often used in the debate on consciousness and AI.

Cognitive bias: the human susceptibility to be swayed by data that is not strictly relevant

Cognitive robots: a UNESCO term for AI that is programmed with algorithms that include learning functionality, which makes their behaviour ultimately unpredictable

Collective Unconscious: a term introduced by Carl Jung to describe that part of the mind that is not directly accessible which seems to be common to humanity as a whole, inherited from our ancestors through evolution; for Jung it is the home of shared mental concepts like the archetypes and folk memories of events like the flood

Connaître: the French verb for knowing that refers to a type of knowing that is subjective, like kennen in German (cf Savoir)

Conscience: the innate human capacity to feel moral qualms

Consciousness: the subjective experience of 'me-ness;' or an ability to experience qualia

Consubstantial, Coeternal: theological jargon for the three distinct persons of the Holy Trinity (God the Father, Son, and Holy Spirit) being at once made of the same substance and existing with each other eternally

Control Problem: how to design AI in such a way that we do not lose control of it

Convolutional neural network: an AI Deep Learning program that uses neural networks for image recognition and processing and is specifically designed to process pixel data

Crystallised Intelligence: Raymond Cattell's theory that one part of human intelligence is the sum total of everything we have learned or know, stored in the brain, which we can access and deploy for problem-solving (cf Fluid Intelligence)

Dead metaphor: a metaphor that is now used as a real descriptor, e.g., electric current or live wire

Deep Blue: the name of the IBM computer that beat the world champion Garry Kasparov in a chess game in 1996

Deep Learning: the use in AI of artificial neural network architectures to establish layers of problem-solving between artificial neurons, with a division of labour by layer, and multiple relationships and iterations between them, to optimise data processing

Deep Mind: the UK company owned by Google which uses Deep Learning in developing a suite of AI tools designed to move towards the development of Artificial General Intelligence

Determinism: the view that all events are determined by previous events or causes (cf Fatalism)

Deterministic robots: a UNESCO term for AI that is programmed with deterministic algorithms which produce predictable behaviour

Dualism, property: the view that the soul is separate from the body not in substance but in the properties that it possesses

Dualism, substance: the view that the soul is made from a different substance than the body

Effective Altruism: a philosophy and community focused on maximising impact through career, projects, and donations, by calculating which causes or problems are important, neglected, and tractable

Eliminativism: the view that consciousness is an illusion and merely an epiphenomenal side-effect of brain functioning

Emergentism: the view that consciousness is a property of matter which spontaneously emerges when a brain gets complex enough (not to be confused with the reverse argument made by Iain McGilchrist, that matter instead emerges from consciousness)

Empiricism: the philosophical view that everything originates in experience, so everything is knowable through experience, which provides the evidence for anything that can be known

Epiphenomenon: a second phenomenon that occurs with or in parallel to a primary phenomenon

Episteme: one of Aristotle's three intellectual virtues (cf Techne and Phronesis) which concerns a person's intelligence about analytical and scientific knowledge and their ability to reason based on analysis and facts

Epistemology: the philosophical study of the nature, origin, and limits of human knowledge

Eucatastrophe: JRR Tolkien's 1939 phrase to describe the joy we feel listening to a story when our hero avoids peril and the story resolves

Eugenics: the process of improving a species or race through selective breeding and intervention

Evolution: the theory that species thrive when they learn and adapt; this gives rise to changes in the heritable characteristics of biological populations over successive generations, such that humans have evolved from earlier species and will continue to change in the future

Executable code: source code that has been compiled in machine code and rendered into a format that makes it operational

Expert System: the milestone in computing that was the introduction of an inference engine twinned with a knowledge base, which for the first time enabled computers to apply rules to facts to deduce new facts or to produce decisions

Fatalism: the belief that all events are determined by previous events or causes and could not turn out in any other way (cf Determinism)

Fluid Intelligence: Raymond Cattell's theory that our other type of human intelligence is an inventive ability to abstract from what we know (cf Crystallised Intelligence) in order to generate fresh insights and novel ideas

Forms: Plato's idea that there are universal perfect versions of the things that exist imperfectly in our world

Ghost in the machine: Gilbert Ryle's 1949 description of his argument that an idealist theory of mind makes a category mistake by considering physical reality as being in the same category as mental reality; and a materialist theory of mind makes the same category mistake by conflating matter and mind which are properly two separate logical categories

Gruffalo Defence: an Ontological Proof for the existence of God that argues (after the story written by Julia Donaldson) that just because we have made something up, it does not follow that the thing we have made up does not also exist

Hamartia: in Greek tragedy, the fatal flaw in a person which makes a tragic outcome inevitable

Hard Problem, the: a reference to the intractable problem of defining consciousness

Hubris: in Greek tragedy, the arrogant overconfidence that courts a tragic turn of events

Hylomorphism: the Aristotelian theory that every being is comprised of matter and form, such that the soul is the form of the body's matter and animates it

I Ching: an ancient Chinese text used for divination; it comprises 64 sets of 'hexagrams' each of which stacks 6 lines that are either broken or unbroken in sequence. They are accompanied by sets of statements which yield the relevant advice in the divination

Idealism: the view that everything is a mental event: everything that exists is either a mind or depends on a mind, because our minds create our reality

Irrealis: types of grammatical mood which relate to things that are not the case, either because they will never be the case or because they are not yet the case, deployed to express things that exist in the realm of thought or the imagination

Jacquard loom: a machine invented by Joseph Marie Jacquard in 1804 that used punched cards to automate complex pattern weaving in cloth manufacture, and provided the inspiration for Charles Babbage's early computer designs

Junk Code: in computing, redundant code that could be deleted or rewritten in shorter syntax without affecting the execution of the program; in this book, those human characteristics that have been deliberately excluded from AI as being irrelevant, distracting, or dangerous, like the emotions, mistakes, story-telling, Sixth Sense, uncertainty, free will, and meaning

Kennen: the German verb for knowing that refers to a type of knowing that is subjective, like connaître in French (cf Wissen)

Language games: a concept invented by Ludwig Wittgenstein to solve the problem of how to talk about things that are not altogether real or known, like a belief in God; which holds that such games are internally consistent and make perfect sense in their own context

Legal Personality: having in law similar rights to a human person to enter into contracts, to sue and be sued, to own property, etc., e.g., a corporation has legal personality

Long Short-term Memory Recurrent Neural Networks (LSTMs): a type of recurrent neural network that can remember and discover the importance of events that happened thousands of processing steps ago, so they are good at sequence prediction problems, like translation and speech recognition, which require long-term as well as short-term memory

Machine Ethics: the emerging field of inquiry into how best to make AI behave ethically

Machine Learning: the general term for the development of algorithms in AI that can improve automatically through experience, built using training data to prime them to make future predictions or decisions without being explicitly programmed to do so

Materialism: the view that matter is all that exists, so mental states and consciousness must also be manifestations of matter

Maxipok: Nick Bostrom's rule of thumb for moral action, which holds that in the face of an existential risk one should maximise the probability of an 'okay outcome,' where an okay outcome is any outcome that avoids existential disaster

Max-Pooling Convolutional Neural Networks: a Deep Learning AI program that combines convolution with pooling to consolidate the learning from each layer of neurons before passing its conclusions on to the other layers, which promotes efficiency by reducing load and noise

Mens rea: the legal jargon for criminal intent, from the Latin for 'guilty mind'

Metaphysics: the branch of philosophy that deals with first principles like the nature of reality, whether or not we exist, and the concepts of time and space; traditionally it has also dealt with the supernatural and the religions, and is the home discipline of mind, consciousness, and soul

Mimetic Desire: a 1961 theory developed by René Girard which holds that we learn by copying both the behaviour of those around us, and their desires

Mind/Brain theory: the area of philosophy concerned with determining the relationship between the physical brain and the (traditionally assumed to be) non-physical mind; generally now positioned as the debate on consciousness

Mission Command: a type of military strategy that establishes hierarchies of objectives to allow rapid readjustment in the field without compromising the superordinate goal

Monism: the view that everything is one thing; there are no divisions

Mood: in grammar, the use of different modes to convey distinctions in language, for instance to indicate whether an utterance is a question, a statement, a hope, or a command

Moore's Law: Gordon Moore's 1965 prediction that the number of transistors on a microchip would double every two years, while the cost of computers would halve

Moravec's Paradox: Hans Moravec's 1988 observation that it is easier to make computers exhibit adult level performance on intelligence tests than it is to give them the skills of a toddler when it comes to perception and mobility

Naturalism: the view that only natural and not supernatural laws and forces are in operation in the universe

Negative Capability: a term coined by the poet John Keats in 1817 to describe the capacity to be in uncertainties, mysteries, and doubts without needing to resolve them through facts and reason

Nemesis: in Greek tragedy, the moment of downfall, when a hero with a fatal flaw, suffering from hubris, meets a crisis and is unable to prevail

Neural Network: in AI, the artificial mimicry in programming of the neural networks of the human brain, used in Deep Learning to accelerate autonomous learning by creating a capacity for complex processing through the use of the neuron layers that define 'deep' learning

Ontogeny non-discrimination: a principle used by Nick Bostrom to argue that if AI had the same functionality and the same conscious experience as a human, then regardless of any difference in how we both came in to being, they would merit equivalent moral status to humans

Ontology: the philosophical study of the nature of reality

Paradigm shift: jargon for step-changes in awareness or understanding such as the Copernican Revolution or Einstein's Theory of Relativity; often used colloquially for any insight that redefines an academic field

Phronesis: one of Aristotle's three intellectual virtues (cf Episteme and Techne) which relates to practical wisdom, value-judgements, and moral choice

Physicalism: the view that everything in existence is physical; nothing else exists

Plea in mitigation: in law, the submissions made by the defendant or their representative as part of the sentencing process, to present any mitigating circumstances that the judge should take into account while sentencing

Predestination: the belief that all the events of your life have already been willed by God

Predetermination: the belief that all the events of your life have been already decided or are already known by whoever or whatever logic it was that designed the world

Psychopathy: a neuro-psychiatric disorder characterised in humans by deficient emotional responses, a lack of empathy, poor behavioural controls, and an absence of conscience or any capacity for remorse. Usually assessed using the Robert D. Hare Psychopathy Checklist.

Qualia: individual instances of subjective, conscious experience (cf Sentience)

Quantum entanglement: Einstein's 'spooky action at a distance' whereby once a particle has interacted with another particle, they will remember that entanglement thereafter, and it will continue to affect their behaviour into the future

Realis: types of grammatical mood which relate to things that are the case, used to portray situations that are real

Recurrent Neural Network: a type of Deep Learning neural network that contains feedback loops to promote the persistence of information over time in order to create 'memory'

Reinforcement Learning: a program that rewards and punishes AI to drive its learning and improvement

Robot: a word first coined in a 1920s science fiction play by the Czech writer Karel Čapek called RUR (Rossum's Universal Robots) and used mainly in literature to describe AI that has been given a physical body which resembles a human person (cf Cognitive and Deterministic Robots)

Robotics: the marriage of computer science and engineering to design machines that can help humans

SF: Science Fiction or Speculative Fiction, used here interchangeably to relate to stories of internally consistent parallel or future worlds that often contain AI and alternative intelligences

Sapience: possessing or having the ability to possess wisdom (cf Sentience)

Savoir: the French verb for knowing that refers to a type of knowing that is objective, like wissen in German (cf Connaître)

Self-awareness: in humans, the ability to have a sense of self; in robots, their existing ability to build a virtual model of their own body in space, and any eventual ability they may develop to build a similar virtual model for their robot 'mind' or artificial intelligence

Sentience: an ability to sense, an ability to perceive, and feel things (cf Sapience; Qualia)

Seven Basic Plots: Christopher Booker's distillation of the world's stories into seven distinct storylines: Overcoming the Monster, Rags to Riches, The Quest, Voyage and Return, Comedy, Tragedy, and Rebirth

Singularity, the: the irreversible point in the future at which AI overtakes human intelligence such that it can no longer be controlled by humankind

Sociopathy: a non-diagnostic term for a neuro-psychiatric disorder that is often confused with psychopathy, except that a sociopath does have a conscience but has managed to suppress it

Sophistry and illusion: David Hume's famous dismissal of metaphysics as an exercise in delusional cleverness

Soul: the idea that we possess an ineffable spirit or vital spark that feels life-giving

Source Code: the basic instructions or design written in text that in programming are then compiled in machine code and operationalised through executable code

Stochastic algorithms: algorithms that include learning functionality, which makes the behaviour of the AI into which they are programmed ultimately unpredictable

Stoicism: an ancient philosophy that teaches the development of self-control and fortitude and the overcoming of destructive emotions:

which are properly errors of judgement: in order to seek happiness in virtue

Substrate Non-Discrimination: a principle used by Nick Bostrom to argue that if AI had the same functionality and the same conscious experience as a human, then regardless of whether they were made of the same substance as a human, they merit equivalent moral status

Techne: one of Aristotle's three intellectual virtues (cf Episteme and Phronesis) which is about applying intelligence to making things, either through materials like wood or clay, or through media like song and dance

Technomoral virtues: a phrase coined by Shannon Vallor to describe the list of virtues that should govern our interaction with AI

Tragedy: the story genre in which a hero with a fatal flaw (hamartia) and full of arrogant overconfidence (hubris) meets a crisis which leads to their downfall (nemesis)

Transistor: a device made from a semiconductor like silicon used in electronics to amplify or switch electrical signals and power

Turing Test: Alan Turing's 1950 suggestion that a computer could be deemed to be 'thinking' if it were able to fool a person into thinking it was a fellow human being, which has become the standard benchmark in AI

UNESCO: the United Nations Educational, Scientific and Cultural Organization, a specialised agency with aims to promote world peace and security through international cooperation in education, arts, sciences, and culture

Uncanny Valley: the hypothesis that humans react in indirect proportion to the verisimilitude of a robot, such that an AI appearing too human will repel rather than attract a human

Utilitarianism: the school of morality often summarised as 'the greatest good for the greatest number' which prioritises outcomes over intent

Vale of soul-making: a phrase coined by the poet John Keats in 1819 and adopted in theodicy by John Hick to describe the formation of moral character through the vicissitudes of life

Veil of Ignorance: John Rawls' 1971 idea that those designing a society should design blind to their own potential status, assuming they might be the losers as well as the winners in any scenario, on the view that this would result in a design that would be fair for everyone

Virtue Ethics: the school of morality that draws on Aristotle to argue for an approach to ethics that focuses on the formation of a person's character rather than the rules governing their individual decisions

Wissen: the German verb for knowing that refers to a type of knowing that is objective, like savoir in French (cf Kennen)

Zero-shot learning: the human capacity to tackle something new, for instance to size up an unfamiliar object and then move it, because of pre-existing spatial self-maps and a general knowledge of how to address such challenges

References

Adams, Douglas (2002) *Life, the Universe and Everything*, London: Picador

Almeida, Patricia, Santos Jr, Carlos & Farias, Josivania (2021) 'Artificial intelligence regulation: a framework for governance,' *Ethics and Information Technology* 23:10

Anderson, Michael & Anderson, Susan Leigh (2011) *Machine Ethics*, Cambridge: CUP

Antognazza, Maria Rosa (ed) (2021) *The Oxford Handbook of Leibniz*, Oxford: OUP

Ariely, Dan (2009) *Predicably Irrational*, London: Harper

Asaro, PM (2012) 'A body to kick, but still no soul to damn: legal perspectives on robotics,' in Lin, P, Abney, K & Bekey, GA, eds, *Robot Ethics*, London: MIT Press, 169–186

Asimov, Isaac (2018) *I Robot*, New York: Harper Voyager

Asimov, Isaac (2018) *Robots and Empire*, New York: Harper Voyager

Avila Negri, Sergio MC (2021) 'Robot as legal person: electronic personhood in robotics and artificial intelligence,' *Frontiers in Robotics and AI*, Volume 8. DOI: 10.3389/frobt.2021.789327

Babiak, Paul & Hare, Robert D (2007) *Snakes in Suits*, New York: HarperCollins

Bakan, Joel (2004) *The Corporation*, London: Constable & Robinson

Bakhtin, A, Brown, N, Dinan, E, Lewis, M et al (2022) 'Human-level play in the game of diplomacy by combining language models with strategic reasoning,' *Science*, 378:6624, 1067–1074

Bash, Anthony (2020) *Remorse*, Eugene, OR: Cascade

Beames, Simon, Mackie, Chris & Scrutton, Roger (2020) 'Alumni perspectives on a boarding school outdoor education programme,' *Journal of Adventure Education and Outdoor Learning*, 20:2, 123–137.

Beck, Richard (2021) *Hunting Magic Eels*, Minneapolis, MN: Broadleaf

Biggar, Nigel (2009), 'Saving the "Secular" – the public vocation of moral theology,' *Journal of Religious Ethics* 37:1, 159–178

Boden MA (1988) *Computer Models of Mind*, Cambridge: CUP

Bok, Sissela (1999) *Lying*, New York: Vintage

Booker, Christopher (2004) *The Seven Basic Plots*, London: Continuum

Bostrom, Nick (2002) 'Existential risks: analyzing human extinction scenarios and related hazards,' *Journal of Evolution and Technology*, 9:1, 15–31

Bostrom, Nick (2013) 'Existential risk prevention as global priority,' *Global Policy* 4:1, 15–31 at https://existential-risk.org/concept.pdf

Bostrom, Nick & Yudkowsky, Eliezer (2014) 'The ethics of artificial intelligence,' in Ramsey W & Frankish, K, eds, *The Cambridge Handbook of Artificial Intelligence*, Cambridge: CUP

Bostrom, Nick (2017) *Superintelligence*, Oxford: OUP

Brand, P & Yancey, P (2010) *Fearfully and Wonderfully Made*, Grand Rapids, MI: Zondervan

Breithaupt, Fritz, Li, Binyan & Kruschke, John (2022) 'Serial reproduction of narratives preserves emotional appraisals,' *Cognition and Emotion* 15, 1–21

Brown, Dan (2017) *Origin*, London: Penguin

Brown, S, Davidovic, J, & Hasan, A (2021) 'The algorithm audit: scoring the algorithms that score us,' *Big Data & Society* 8:1, 1–8

Brown, ZC, Anicich, EM, & Galinsky, AD (2020) 'Compensatory conspicuous communication: low status increases jargon use,' *Organizational Behavior and Human Decision Processes* 161, 274–290.

Bungay, Stephen (2011) *The Art of Action*, Boston, MA: Nicholas Brealey

Burns, JM & Swerdlow, RH (2003) 'Right orbitofrontal tumor with pedophilia symptom and constructional apraxia sign,' *Archives of Neurology* 60:3, 437–440

Carr, M, Curd, J & Dent, F (2005) *MBTI Research into Distribution of Type*, Berkhamsted: Ashridge Business School

Carroll, Lewis (1910) *Through the Looking Glass and What Alice Found There*, London: Macmillan

Caruso, Gregg D (2022) 'The public health-quarantine model,' in the *Oxford Handbook of Moral Responsibility*, Nelkin, D & Pereboom, D, eds, New York: OUP, 222–246

Cattell, RB (1963) 'Theory of fluid and crystallized intelligence: a critical experiment,' *Journal of Educational Psychology* 54, 1–22

Chen, B, Kwiatkowski, R, Vondrick, C & Lipson, H (2022) 'Fully body visual self-modeling of robot morphologies,' *Science Robotics*, 7:68, eabn1944

Chiang, Ted (2002) *Stories of Your Life and Others*, London: Picador

Chiang, Ted (2019) *Exhalation*, London: Picador

Christian, Brian (2020) *The Alignment Problem*, London: Atlantic Books

Coates, JM, Gurnell, M, & Sarnyai, Z (2010) 'From molecule to market: steroid hormones and financial risk-taking,' *Philosophical Transactions of the Royal Society B Biological Sciences* 365:1538, 331–43

Coleridge, ST (1997) *The Complete Poems of Samuel Taylor Coleridge*, London: Penguin

COMEST report on Robotics Ethics at https://unesdoc.unesco.org/ark:/48223/pf0000253952

Corcoran, K, ed (2001) *Soul, Body, and Survival*, Ithaca, NY: Cornell University Press

Cottingham, John (2020) *In Search of the Soul*, Princeton, NJ: Princeton University Press

Criado Perez, Caroline (2019) *Invisible Women*, London: Vintage

Davies, Robertson (1983) *The Deptford Trilogy*, London: Penguin

Dennett, Daniel C (1988) 'Quining qualia,' in Marcel, A & Bisiach, E, eds, *Consciousness in Modern Science*, Oxford: OUP

Dennett, Daniel C (1993) *Consciousness Explained*, London: Penguin

Denno, D (2011) 'Courts' increasing consideration of behavioral genetics evidence in criminal cases,' *Michigan State Law Review*, 967, 967–1047. https://core.ac.uk/download/pdf/144231854.pdf

DeYoung, CG, Hirsh, JB, Shane, MS, Papademetris, X, Rajeevan, N. & Gray, JR (2010) 'Testing predictions from personality neuroscience: brain structure and the Big Five,' *Psychological Science*, 21:6, 820–828

Dickins, Rosie (2015) *Computers and Coding*, London: Usborne

Dorobantu, Marius (2021) 'Cognitive vulnerability, artificial intelligence, and the image of god in humans,' *Journal of Disability & Religion*, 25:1, 27–40

Dreyfus, Hubert L (1992) *What Computers Still Can't Do*, Cambridge, MA: MIT press

Dreyfus, Hubert L (2007) 'Why Heideggerian AI failed and how fixing it would require making it more Heideggerian,' *Artificial Intelligence* 171:18, 1137–1160

Ekman, Paul (1999), 'Basic emotions,' in Dalgleish, T, & Power, M, eds, *Handbook of Cognition and Emotion*, Chichester: Wiley

Fine, G (1983) 'Plato and Aristotle on form and substance,' *Proceedings of the Cambridge Philological Society*, 29, 23–47

Fjeld, Jessica, Achten, Nele, Hilligoss, Hannah, Nagy, Adam, & Srikumar, Madhu (2020), 'Principled artificial intelligence: mapping consensus in ethical and rights-based approaches to principles for AI,' Berkman Klein Center for Internet & Society

Flyvbjerg, Bent (2002) *Making Social Science Matter*, Cambridge: CUP

Foster, Charles (2021) *Being A Human*, London: Profile

Foster, Claire & Newell, Edmund, eds (2005) *The Worlds We Live In*, London: Darton, Longman & Todd.

Frankl, Viktor E (2004) *Man's Search for Meaning*, London: Rider

Fuegi, John & Francis, John (2003) 'Lovelace & Babbage and the creation of the 1843 "notes,"' *IEEE Annals of the History of Computing* 25:4, 16–26

Fukushima, K (1980) 'Neocognitron: a self-organizing neural network model for a mechanism of pattern recognition unaffected by shift in position,' *Biological Cybernetics*, 36, 193–202

Furnham, A, Mouttafi, J, & Crump, J (2003) 'The relationship between the revised NEO-personality inventory and the Myers-Briggs type indicator,' *Social Behavior and Personality*, 31:6, 577–584

Gaita, Raimond (2002) *A Common Humanity*, London & New York: Routledge

Gambetta, Diego & Hertog, Steffen (2016) *Engineers of Jihad*, Princeton, NJ: Princeton University Press

Gawdat, Mo (2021) *Scary Smart*, London: Bluebird

Geraci, RM (2006) 'Spiritual robots: religion and our scientific view of the natural world,' *Theology and Science*, 4:3, 229–246.

Giorgi, S, Le Nguyen, K, Eichstaedt, JC, Kern, ML, Yaden, DB, Kosinski, M, Seligman, MEP, Ungar, LH, Schwartz, HA, & Park, G (2021) 'Regional personality assessment through social media language,' *Journal of Personality* 90:3, 405–425

Gladwell, Malcolm (2006) *Blink*, London: Penguin

Glattfelder, James B (2019) *Information—Consciousness—Reality*, New York: Springer

Goetz, S & Taliaferro, C (2011) *A Brief History of the Soul*, Chichester: Wiley-Blackwell

Goleman, Daniel (1996) *Emotional Intelligence*, London: Bloomsbury

Gooder, Paula (2016) *Body*, London: SPCK

Gosling, SD, Rentfrow, PJ & Swann, WB Jr (2005) 'A very brief measure of the Big-Five personality domains,' *Journal of Research in Personality* 37; 504–528.

Graziano, Michael (2018) *The Spaces Between Us: A Story of Neuroscience, Evolution, and Human Nature*, New York: OUP

Guiso, Luigi, Sapienza, Paola & Zingales, Luigi (2003) 'People's opium? Religion and economic attitudes,' *Journal of Monetary Economics* 50:1, 225–282

Gunkel, David J (2018) *Robot Rights*, Cambridge, MA: MIT Press

Hallie, Philip (1985) 'Classical scepticism—a polemical introduction,' in Hallie, Phillip, ed, *Sextus Empiricus: Selections from the Major Writings on Scepticism, Man, and God*, Indianapolis, IN: Hackett

Haraway, Donna (1985) 'A manifesto for cyborgs: science, technology, and socialist feminism in the 1980s,' *Socialist Review* 80

Harris, Sam (2012) *Free Will*, New York: Free Press

Hick, John (1991) *Evil and the God of Love*, Basingstoke: Macmillan

Hicks, RD (1907) *Aristotle's De Anima*, Cambridge: CUP

Hinton, GE, Osindero, S, & Teh, Y-W (2006) 'A fast learning algorithm for deep belief nets,' *Neural Computation*, 18:7, 1527–1554

Hobbes, Thomas (2017) *Leviathan*, London: Penguin

Hodges, Andrew (2014) *Alan Turing: The Enigma*, London: Vintage

Hood, Robert E (1994) *Begrimed and Black*, Minneapolis, MN: Fortress Press

Hume, David (1999) *An Enquiry Concerning Human Understanding*, Oxford: OUP

Inglehart, Ronald F (2021) *Religion's Sudden Decline: What's Causing It, and What Comes Next?* New York: OUP

Ishiguro, Kazuo (2021), *Klara and the Sun*, London: Faber & Faber

James, Oliver (2007) *Affluenza*, London: Vermillion

James, Oliver (2008) *The Selfish Capitalist*, London: Vermillion

Kahneman, Daniel (2012) *Thinking Fast and Slow*, London: Penguin

Keats, John (2009) *Selected Letters*, Oxford: OUP

Koenig-Robert, R, Pearson, J (2019) 'Decoding the contents and strength of imagery before volitional engagement,' *Scientific Reports* 9, 3504

Konadu, DD, Mourão, ZS, Allwood, JM, Richards, KS, Kopec, G, McMahon, R, & Fenner, R (2015) 'Land use implications of future energy system trajectories' *Energy Policy* 86, 328–337

Kramm, Matthias (2020) 'When a river becomes a person,' *Journal of Human Development and Capabilities* 21:4, 307–319

Larkin, Philip (1964) *The Whitsun Weddings*, London: Faber & Faber

Layard, Richard (2005) *Happiness*, London: Penguin

Lewis, CS (2002) *Mere Christianity*, London: Harper Collins

Lodge, David (2002) *Thinks*, London: Penguin

Logg, JM, Minson, JA & Moore, DA (2019) 'Algorithm appreciation: people prefer algorithmic to human judgment,' *Organizational Behavior and Human Decision Processes* 151, 90–103

Loiacono, D, Lanzi, PL, Togelius, J, Onieva, E, Pelta, DA, Butz, MV, Lonneker, TD, Cardamone, L, Perez, D, Saez, Y, Preuss, M, & Quadflieg, J (2010) 'The 2009 simulated car racing championship,' *IEEE Transactions on Computational Intelligence and AI in Games*, 2:2

MacAskill, William (2015) *Doing Good Better*, London: Guardian Books and Faber & Faber

MacDougall, Duncan (1907) 'Hypothesis concerning soul substance together with experimental evidence of the existence of such a substance,' *Journal of the American Society for Psychical Research* 1:5, 237–275

Machiavelli, Niccolo (1995) *The Prince*, trans George Bull, London: Penguin

Martinón-Torres, M, d'Errico, F, Santos, E et al (2021) 'Earliest known human burial in Africa' *Nature* 593, 95–100

McEwan, Ian (2020) *Machines Like Me*, London: Vintage

McGilchrist, Iain (2009) *The Master and His Emissary*, New Haven, CT: Yale University Press

McGilchrist, Iain (2021) *The Matter With Things*, London: Perspectiva

Millbank, Paul (2022) 'A society without imagination: A lament,' *The Kenarchy Journal* 3:1. https://kenarchy.org/starting-points-health-and-wellbeing/

Moravec, Hans (1988) *Mind Children*, Harvard, MA: Harvard University Press

Morse, SJ (1994) 'Culpability and control,' *University of Pennsylvania Law Review* 142, 1587–1660

Morse, SJ (2011) 'Genetics and criminal responsibility,' *Trends in Cognitive Science*, 15:9; 378–380

Moser-Wellman, Annette (2002) *Five Faces of Genius*, New York: Penguin

Myers, IB, McCaulley, MH, Quenk, NL, & Hammer, AL (1998) *MBTI Manual* 3rd Edition, Palo Alto, CA: CPP

Nagel, Thomas (1974) 'What is it like to be a bat?' *The Philosophical Review* 83:4, 435–450

Nagel, Thomas (2012) *Mind and Cosmos*, Oxford: OUP

Nietzsche, Friedrich (1997) *Thus Spake Zarathustra*, trans Anthony Common, Ware: Wordsworth

Nixon, Matt (2016) *Pariahs*, Farringdon: Libri

Onen, M, Emond, N, Wang, B, Zhang, D, Ross, FM, Li, J, Yildiz, B, del Alamo, JA (2022) 'Nanosecond protonic programmable resistors for analog deep learning,' *Science* 377:6605, 539–543

Palmer, FR (1973) *Grammar*, Harmondsworth: Pelican

Palmer, FR (2001) *Mood and Modality*, Cambridge: CUP

Papadopoulos, Renos K, ed (2006) *The Handbook of Jungian Psychology*, London: Routledge

Pasquale, Frank (2020) *New Laws of Robotics: Defending Human Expertise in the Age of AI*, Harvard, MA: Belknap Press

Perline, IH & Goldschmidt, J (2004) *The Psychology and Law of Workplace Violence*, Springfield, IL: Charles C. Thomas

Perolat, J, De Vylder, B, Tuyls, K et al (2022) 'Mastering the game of Stratego with model-free multiagent reinforcement learning' *Science*, 378:6623, 990–996

Picard, Rosalind (1997) *Affective Computing*, Cambridge, MA: MIT Press

Poetry House (2020) *150 Most Famous Poems*, Springville, UT: Vervante

Poole, Eve (2009) 'Organisational spirituality,' *Journal of Business Ethics* 84:4, 577–588

Poole, Eve (2015) *Capitalism's Toxic Assumptions*, London: Bloomsbury

Poole, Eve (2017) *Leadersmithing*, London: Bloomsbury

Poole, Eve (2018) *Buying God*, London: SCM Press

Prinzing, M, Van Cappellen, P, & Fredrickson, BL (2021) 'More than a momentary blip in the universe?' *Personality and Social Psychology Bulletin* 49:2

Rawls, John (2005) *A Theory of Justice*, Harvard, MA: Harvard University Press

Rhodes, Richard (2012) *Hedy's Folly*, New York: Vintage

Riddell, Patricia (2017) 'Reward and threat in the adolescent brain: implications for leadership,' *Leadership & Organization Development Journal*, 38:4, 530–548

Roux, L, Racoceanu, D, Lomenie, N, Kulikova, M, Irshad, H, Klossa, J, Capron, F, Genestie, C, Naour, GL, & Gurcan, MN (2013) 'Mitosis detection in breast cancer histological images - an ICPR 2012 contest,' *Journal of Pathology Informatics*, 4:8. doi: 10.4103/2153-3539.112693

Russell, Stuart (2020) *Human Compatible*, London: Penguin

Ryle, Gilbert (1990) *The Concept of Mind*, London: Penguin

Schmidhuber, Jürgen (2007) 'Gödel machines: fully self-referential optimal universal self-improvers,' *Cognitive Technologies*, 8:199–226

Schmidhuber, Jürgen (2015) 'Deep learning in neural networks: an overview,' *Neural Networks*, 61, 85–117

Schulz, Kathryn (2010) *Being Wrong*, London: Granta

Searle, John R (1980) 'Minds, brains, and programs' *The Behavioral and Brain Sciences* 3, 417–457

Searle, John R (1999) 'The Chinese room,' in Wilson RA and Keil F, eds, *The MIT Encyclopedia of the Cognitive Sciences*, Cambridge, MA: MIT Press

Searle, John R (2004) *Mind*, Oxford: OUP

Sermanet, P & LeCun, Y (2011) 'Traffic sign recognition with multi-scale convolutional networks,' *Proceedings of the International Joint Conference on Neural Networks*, 2809–2813. doi: 10.1109/IJCNN.2011.6033589.

Smith, Joshua K (2021) *Robotic Persons*, Bloomington, IN: WestBow Press

Smith, Joshua K (2022) *Robot Theology*, Eugene, OR: Wipf & Stock

Song, Robert 'Robots, AI and human uniqueness,' in Wyatt, John & Williams, Stephen N, eds (2021) *The Robot Will See You Now*, London: SPCK

Soon, C, Brass, M, Heinze, HJ et al (2008) 'Unconscious determinants of free decisions in the human brain,' *Nature Neuroscience* 11, 543–545

Soskice, JM (1985) *Metaphor and Religious Language*, Oxford: Clarendon Press

Spufford, Francis (2012) *Unapologetic*, London: Faber & Faber

Stephenson, Neal (1996) *The Diamond Age*, London: Penguin

Stephenson, Neal (2008) *Anathem*, London: Atlantic

Stephenson, Neal (2012) *Some Remarks,* London: Atlantic Books

Stoppard, Tom (2015) *The Hard Problem*, London: Faber

Stump, E (2003) *Aquinas*, New York: Routledge

Sutton, RS, Barto, AG, & Bach, F (2018) *Reinforcement Learning: An Introduction –* 2nd Edition, Cambridge, MA: MIT Press

Taylor, SE, Klein, LC, Lewis, BP, Gruenewald, TL, Gurung, RAR, & Updegraff, JA (2000) 'Biobehavioral responses to stress in females: tend-and-befriend, not fight-or-flight', *Psychological Review*, 107:3, 411–429

Tegmark, Max (2017) *Life 3.0*, London: Penguin

Tenner, Edward (1997) *Why Things Bite Back*, New York: Vintage Books

Thomson JAK (1965) *Aristotle's Nichomachean Ethics*, London: Penguin

Thomson, JAK (1965) *The Ethics of Aristotle*, London: Penguin

Tinwell, Angela (2014) *The Uncanny Valley in Games and Animation*, Boca Raton, FL: CRC Press

Tolkien, JRR (2009) *Tree and Leaf*, London: HarperCollins

Turing, AM (1950) 'Computing machinery and intelligence', *Mind* 59, 433–460

Vallor, Shannon (2016) *Technology and the Virtues*, Oxford: OUP

Wallach, Wendell & Allen, Colin (2009) *Moral Machines*, Oxford: OUP

Wallach, Wendell & Asaro, Peter, eds (2017) *Machine Ethics and Robot Ethics*, London: Routledge

Watson, Richard (2016) *Digital VS Human*, London: Scribe

Weng, J, Ahuja, N, & Huang, TS (1992) 'Cresceptron: a self-organizing neural network which grows adaptively', *International Joint Conference on Neural Networks*, 1, 576–581.

Whitehead, AN (1929) *Process and Reality*, Cambridge: CUP

Williams, Stephen N 'Behind artificial intelligence', in Wyatt, John & Williams, Stephen N, eds (2021) *The Robot Will See You Now*, London: SPCK

Wittgenstein, Ludwig (1980) *Remarks on the Philosophy of Psychology 1*, trans Anscombe, GEM, Chicago, IL: University of Chicago Press

Wittgenstein, Ludwig (1958) *Philosophical Investigations*, trans Anscombe, GEM, Oxford: Blackwell

Wittgenstein, Ludwig (2016) *Tractatus Logico-Philosophicus*, trans Ogden, CK, Asheville, NC: Chiron Academic Press

Woodhead, LJP (2016) 'The Rise of 'No Religion' in Britain: the emergence of a new cultural majority', *Journal of the British Academy* 4, 245–261

Wyatt, John & Williams, Stephen N, eds (2021) *The Robot Will See You Now*, London: SPCK

Yudkowsky, Eliezer (2004) *Coherent Extrapolated Volition*, San Francisco, CA: Machine Intelligence Research Institute

Index

Note: Page numbers followed by "n" denote endnotes.

5, Big Five Personality Traits 54, 56, 118, 138
5 Faces of Genius (Moser-Wellman) 85–86
7 Basic Plots (Booker) 80–82, 121, 131, 146
7 Factors Affecting Happiness (Layard) 91–92
12 scenarios *see* Dooms, the 12 (Tegmark)
21 grams, the weight of the soul (MacDougall) 65
1984 *see* Dooms, the 12 (Tegmark)

a priori 53
accountability 18–19, 21, 22
acedia 91, 137
actuality 66
Adam (McEwen character) 73
Adams, Douglas 118
Affective Computing 116
Affluenza 91, 137
agent, agency 15, 16, 19, 21, 35, 74, 79, 89–90, 106–107, 124
AGI, artificial general intelligence 30, 137
Agnosticism 137
agreeableness *see* the Big Five
AI *see* Artificial Intelligence
Alchemist *see* 5 Faces of Genius
algebra 4
Algocracy 22, 137
algorithm 2, 4, 5, 8, 17, 22–23, 53, 56, 111, 115, 137, 146
  algorithmic bias 17, 23, 53, 56, 115
alien 70, 89, 91
Alignment Problem, the 9, 19, 113, 125, 137
Allegory of the Cave 65
AlphaFold 7, 137; *see also* proteins

AlphaGo 3, 7, 46, 69, 137; *see also* Go
Amazon 53
ambiguity 87–88, 106; *see also* uncertainty
Amusement *see* Ekman's Basic Emotions
amygdalae 76–77, 79
analytic, reasoning 53, 57, 141
Anathem, novel 96n35
android 2, 118
  Marvin the Paranoid Android 118
Anger *see* Ekman's Basic Emotions
animal 16, 20, 73, 83, 130
  animal rights 16
animus 66
Anthropocene 131, 137
Anthropomorphise 16, 20, 22
Anxiety *see* Big Five
Apple 86
application *see* programming
Aquinas 67, 91
archetypes 80–81, 121, 137, 139; *see also* Jung
Arendt, Hannah 111
Aristotle 57–58, 66–67, 81, 119, 141, 145, 147, 148
Armageddon *see* the 12 Dooms
Arrival (movie) 89
arrow 132
artificial intelligence i, xi, xiii, 1–3, 5, 7–11, 15–25, 29–35, 42, 44–47, 51–54, 56–59, 66–71, 74–79, 83, 85–88, 93, 99, 101, 106–109, 112–125, 130–131, 133, 135, 137; *see also* ethics, regulation
  AI consciousness xi, 2, 16, 21, 45–47, 59, 69, 101, 115, 124, 131, 133

artificial intelligence (*cont.*)
  as a focus for EA 112
  Bayesian AI 9, 59, 87–88, 120, 122,
    131, 138
  history 2–11
  legal status 15–17, 20–22, 123
  in SciFi 2, 17, 30–32, 74, 81, 132
  training on games 7, 8, 9
arts, importance of 104, 106, 108
Arundel Tomb 75
ASI, Artificial Super Intelligence 138
Asimov, Isaac 17, 23–24, 138
  Asimov's Rules 17, 24, 138
aspect perception (Wittgenstein) 83
audit, of algorithms 8, 22–23
Augustine 67
authentication 10, 20
Autism 116–117, 138
automata 2
autonomy 16, 19, 88
autopilot 79
Avila Negri, Sergio MC 16, 22

Babbage, Charles 3
Bakan, Joel 22
Bash, Anthony 78, 103
bat, batness 43
Bayes, Bayesian 5, 9, 59, 87, 88, 120, 122,
    131, 138
Beames, Simon 101–103
Beck, Richard 92
Benevolent Dictator *see* the 12 Dooms
bias, biased 17, 23, 42, 53, 55–58, 71n1,
    82, 85, 88, 103, 106, 114–115,
    125, 139
big five, personality traits 54–57, 118, 138
Biggar, Nigel 106
binary 3, 4, 138
binding problem 41
biology, biological 6–7, 16, 20, 29, 33–35,
    39, 56, 83, 118
biomimicry 86
blame 22, 35–36
Bletchley Park 130
Blue Fairy 2
blue, missing shade of 82, 85, 138
Boden, MA 45

Booker, Christopher 80–82, 121, 131
Boole, George 4
  Boolean algebra 4
Bostrom, Nick 15, 16, 24, 68, 71, 112–113,
    143, 144, 147
Box *see* Chinese Room
brain 2, 6, 35–36, 40–43, 45–47, 56–57, 65,
    68–69, 74, 76–77, 79, 83–84, 87,
    89, 100, 121, 130, 138, 140, 144
  left hemisphere 41–42, 105, 138
  right hemisphere 41–42, 87, 138
burials 74–75

calculating machine 3–4, 130
calculations 3, 5, 33, 59, 119–120
calculus 130
Cambridge Analytica 54
camels 73
cancer 6, 130
capability, negative (Keats) 86–87, 144
CAPTCHA 10, 139
car, self-driving 6, 8, 59
Carroll, Lewis 87
Cartesian 67, 139
Caruso, Gregg D 36
category error, category mistake 16, 43, 46,
    53, 139, 141
Cattell, Raymond B 58, 121, 140, 141
causation 36, 68, 89
character, human 67, 78–79, 82, 101–104,
    107, 117, 119, 120, 147, 148;
    see also virtue ethics
character recognition 6
chatbot 8, 10; *see also* Tay
ChatGPT 52; *see also* GPT tools
chess 3, 7, 8, 140; *see also* Deep Blue
Chiang, Ted 89
China 3, 7, 17, 142
Chinese Room 10, 44–47, 51–52, 57–58, 69,
    83, 139
chip, microchip 4
Christian, Brian 9, 111, 118, 122–123
Cicero (AI) 12n23; *see also* Diplomacy
Cinderella 80
citizenship 2, 21, 32
cloning 33
Coates, JM 115

code, coding i, xi, 3, 4, 8, 19, 33, 70, 74,
    79, 83, 93, 99, 101, 108, 109, 112,
    115–116, 118–119, 121–123, 125,
    130–133, 141, 142, 146; *see also*
    junk code
  coding soul 115–124
cogito ergo sum (Descartes) 67
cognitive 2, 5, 20, 54, 85, 124, 137, 139, 146
  bias 85, 139
  robots 5, 124, 139
Coherent Extrapolated Volition 120
Coleridge, ST 83
collective unconscious 47, 81, 94, 105, 122,
    137, 139
Comedy *see* 7 Basic Plots
Commission
  European 21
  sins of 77
  UNESCO 21–22, 124, 139, 140, 147
competencies 30, 88, 100, 116–117
computation, computational 3, 7, 47, 57
computer, computers 3–5, 7, 9–10, 20,
    29–30, 32–33, 44–45, 51, 57, 69,
    73–74, 79, 83
computing 4, 42, 116, 120–121, 130
conflict *see* war
connaître, cf savoir 70, 139, 142, 146
Conquerors *see* the 12 Dooms
conscience 78, 89, 94, 95n20, 101, 119, 133,
    139, 145, 146
conscientiousness *see* the big five
conscious 16, 30, 39–47, 59, 76, 81–82, 125
consciousness i, xi, 2, 16, 39–47, 52, 59,
    64–71, 74, 81, 89–90, 101, 115,
    124, 131, 133, 139, 140, 142,
    143, 144
consubstantial, coeternal 88, 139
Contempt *see* Ekman's Basic Emotions
Contentment *see* Ekman's Basic Emotions
contingent 53
control, controls i, xi, 6, 8, 15,
    18–19, 23–25, 30–32, 36,
    112–113, 125, 140
  control problem, the i, 19, 23–24,
    32, 140
convolutional neural network 6, 59n2,
    140, 143

copy, copying 30, 42, 44, 70, 74, 107,
    133, 144
corporation 21–22
  legal personality of 21–22, 143
corporeality 67
cortex 5, 56
Cottingham, John 132
Covid-19 87, 105; *see also* pandemic
creativity 58, 85–86, 122–123
Cresceptron 6, 59n2
Criado Perez, Caroline 114
crime, criminal 36, 107, 143
crystallised intelligence (Cattell), cf fluid
    intelligence 58, 122, 140
curricula 19, 100–102, 108
Curriculum, for Happiness (Layard) 108
cyborg, cyborgs 31, 113
  Cyborg Manifesto (Haraway) 113–114

Darwin, Charles 75, 77
data, datasets xi, 1, 4–5, 9–10, 17–18, 23,
    46, 53–59, 69, 75, 84–85, 87, 91,
    93, 99, 100
Davies, Robertson 95n23
decrypted 4
Deep Blue 37, 140
Deep Learning 1, 5–9, 30, 46, 59, 116, 123,
    140, 143, 144, 145
Deep Mind 7, 137, 140
DeepNash 12n23; *see also* Stratego
definitions *see* glossary
Dennett, Daniel C 44, 68
Descartes, Rene 67, 109, 139
Descendents *see* the 12 Dooms
design, human i, xi, 64, 66, 70, 74, 77–78,
    86, 90–91, 94, 108, 115
determinism 90, 140
deterministic robots 5, 124, 140
digital 4, 19, 138
dignity xi, 19, 33, 124
Diplomacy 12n23; *see also* Cicero (AI)
disability 33
discrimination 16, 18, 144, 147;
    see also bias
Disgust *see* Ekman's Basic Emotions
Disney 75
distinctiveness 32–33, 39, 59, 76, 80, 90, 131

distress *see* Ekman's Basic Emotions
divination 142; *see also* I Ching
DNA 33, 35–36, 70
Doctor Who 70, 133
Dooms, the 12 (Tegmark) 30–32, 112
Dorobantu, Marius 97n65
drones 17
dualism 64–66, 140
duck/rabbit illusion 83, 130

EA *see* Effective Altruism
education 19, 30, 94, 100–103, 105, 147
Effective Altruism 112–113, 140
Egalitarian Utopia *see* the 12 Dooms
Einstein, Albert 40–41, 47, 145
Ekman's Basic Emotions 76
Ekman, Paul 75–76, 116
electronic personhood 21–22
Eliminativism, eliminativists
    65–66, 68, 140
Embarrassment *see* Ekman's Basic
    Emotions
emergence 2, 39
Emergentism, emergentists 65, 69, 140
emotions 16, 21, 41, 74, 75, 76, 94, 100–101,
    116–118
emotional intelligence 100, 103, 105,
    116–117, 122–124
empathy, empathetic 55, 117, 145
empiricism, empiricist 39, 42, 53, 56, 82, 141
enchantment 92
engine, search 10
Enigma 4
Enlightenment 32, 87
Enslaved God *see* the 12 Dooms
entanglement, quantum 47, 121, 145
epiphenomenon, epiphenomenal
    65, 140, 141
episteme 57–59, 141
epistemological 56–57
epistemology, epistemologies 47, 51–53, 55,
    57, 59, 70, 141
err, error 6, 8, 23, 36, 53, 58, 69, 74, 77–78,
    88, 94, 118, 122
eternity 78, 90
    eternity's emissaries (Kierkegaard) 78
ethical, ethically 19, 23, 32, 68, 78, 109,
    118–119, 124, 143

ethics 5, 15–19, 21, 57, 90, 101, 107,
    118–120, 143, 148
    Machine 119, 143
    Nicomachean 57, 119
    public 32
    robot 15, 119
    virtue 90, 107, 119, 148
EU 17, 21, 23
eucatastrophe 82–83, 132–133, 141
eugenics 33–35, 141
eureka 73, 83
evidence 36, 52–53, 112, 141
evil 73, 80
evolution, evolutionary 2–3, 7, 29–30, 39,
    43–44, 46, 64, 69, 70, 75–77,
    80–81, 93, 132, 141
Excitement *see* Ekman's Basic Emotions
executable code 70, 141, 146
expert system 4, 141
explainability 18, 22–23
extraversion *see* the Big Five; MBTI
Ezekiel 64

Facebook 54
facial recognition 20, 116
Factors *see* 7 Factors Affecting Happiness
fairness 18–19, 34–35
faith 19, 41–42, 64, 84, 87–88, 93, 108,
    113, 137
falsifiable 40, 64
fatal flaw 131–132, 142, 144, 147
fatalism 90, 141
fear *see* Ekman's Basic Emotions
feeling *see* MBTI
femur 69
Fermat's principle of least time 89
fiction, fictional 17, 30, 32, 52, 73–74,
    81, 104, 118, 121, 132; *see also*
    storytelling
Fjeld, Jessica 18
flaw, fatal 131–132, 142, 144, 147
fluid intelligence (Cattell), cf crystallised
    intelligence 58–59, 84, 141
Flyvbjerg, Bent 58
folklore, myth 2, 64, 80–81, 115, 121,
    132, 139
foodbanks 107
fool *see* 5 Faces of Genius

form, forms 65–66, 71, 74, 131–132, 141
Formula 1, F1 86
FORTRAN 4
Foster, Charles 33, 40
foveal vision 83
Frankl, Viktor E 90
free will 35–36, 74, 79, 88–91, 93, 100–101,
        106–108, 118, 123–124, 132
freedom xi, 19, 21, 79, 89–90, 92, 106, 108,
        123
Freud, Sigmund 81
Fukushima, K 6

Gambetta, Diego 106
games, gaming 6–10, 12n21–25, 20, 30, 40,
        68, 87, 114, 121, 123, 130, 133,
        140, 143
game theory 8, 114
gamification 89
gasmask 70–71
gatekeeper see the 12 Dooms
Gawdat, Mo 112
gender 34, 46, 53, 55, 75, 100, 103, 105,
        114–115
genes, genetics 29, 33–34, 35–36, 40
genocide 33
Geraci, RM 71n1, 72n11
Ghost in the Machine (Ryle) 43, 141
Girard, Rene 107, 144
Gladwell, Malcolm 82
glossary 137–148
Go 7, 30, 69, 137; see also AlphaGo
God, gods 2, 31, 42, 63–65, 67–68, 73,
        78–79, 88, 92, 111, 123, 129, 132,
        137, 138, 139, 142, 143, 145
Godel Machine (Schmidhuber) 8
Goetz, S 64
Goleman, Daniel 100, 116
Google 7, 10, 44, 58, 140
Gordonstoun i, 102
governing, governance 17, 125; see also
        regulation
GPT tools xiii, 52
GPUs 6
Graziano, Michael 69
Great Ormond Street Hospital 86
grief 75
Gruffalo Defence 64, 142

Guillotine (Hume) 60n7
guilt, guilty 35, 76, 78–79, 143; see also
        Ekman's Basic Emotions
Gunkel, David J 15

hackers, hacking 10, 18, 74
Hahn, Kurt 101–102
hamartia 131–132, 142
handwriting recognition 6, 44–45
happiness 31, 58, 76–77, 91–92, 108, 117,
        147; see also Ekman's Basic
        Emotions
        7 factors affecting 91–92
Haraway, Donna 15, 113–114
Hard Problem (play) 40
Hard Problem, the 40, 47, 142
hardware 3–4
Hare, Robert D 22, 145; see also
        psycopathy scale
Harris, Sam 89
Harry Potter 82, 85
Hawking, Stephen 29–30
hemispheres, of the brain (McGilchrist)
        41–42, 87, 105, 138
Hertog, Steffen 106
Hesiod 2
Heuristics 120
hexagrams 3, 142; see also I Ching
Hick, John 78–79, 147
Higgs boson 57
Hinton, GE 5
hippogriff 83
Hobbes, Thomas 3, 42, 57–58
holy 84, 88, 139
HPtFtU 78, 95n12
hubris 131, 142, 144, 147
human
        design i, xi, 64, 66, 70, 74, 77–78, 86,
                90–91, 94, 108, 115
        error 6, 8, 23, 36, 53, 58, 69, 74, 77–78,
                88, 94, 118, 122
        extinction 31–32, 112
        intelligence 10, 15, 30–31, 51–59, 79, 84,
                122, 125, 133, 140, 141
        intervention 4, 9, 141
        obsolescence 29–30, 32, 74
        preferences 24, 54–56, 117
        rights xi, 21, 67, 106

human (*cont.*)
　skills 19, 30, 57, 94, 103, 119 (*see also* competencies)
　soul xi, 2, 42–43, 59, 63–71, 74, 78–79, 84–85, 91, 93, 109, 112, 115, 124, 129, 131–133, 135, 137, 140, 142, 143, 146, 147
　values i, 18–19, 68, 80, 91–92, 99, 108–109, 119–120
humanity i, xi, 17–18, 25, 31, 35, 66–67, 78, 81, 88, 90–92, 99, 104, 106, 108, 111–125, 130, 133
humanoid 2
Hume, David 39, 40, 82, 138, 146
hylomorphism 66, 142

I Ching 3, 142; *see also* divination
I Robot (Asimov) 17, 26n8
IBM 4, 7, 140
idealism 65, 142
image recognition 6, 140
imagination 2, 10, 41, 55–56, 82–84, 87, 100, 104, 107, 142
immortal, soul 65
impartial observer (Smith) 78
imperative mood 53, 87
Intel 4
interface, biomimicry 86
internet 7, 18, 30, 52, 58
interrogative mood 87
introversion *see* MBTI
intuition i, 5, 41, 55, 65, 82, 84, 91, 94, 117, 121; *see also* MBTI and Sixth Sense
intuitive 4–5, 21, 41, 65, 117
irrationality 74, 77
irrealis moods 87, 142
is/ought (Hume's Guillotine) 60n7

Jacquard looms 3, 142
jam experiment 107
James, Oliver 91
Japan 2, 6, 9, 122
Jargon 51, 59n1, 68; *see also* Glossary
Jaws 80
Joy *see* Ekman's Basic Emotions
Judging *see* MBTI
Jung, Carl 55, 81, 137, 139

Junk Code i, xi, 71, 73–94, 99–100, 104, 109, 111, 115, 123–125, 130–132, 135, 142
justice 34–35, 124

Kahneman, Daniel 82
Keats, John 79, 86, 144, 147
Kennen, cf Wissen 72n18, 142
Kierkegaard, Soren 78
kill switch 8–9
knowing, ways of 51–53, 57–59
Kosinski, M 54

Lamarr, Hedy 83
LaMDA 10
language 3–6, 16, 24, 40–41, 43–45, 47, 80, 83, 87, 89, 130, 144
　language games 40, 68, 121, 130, 143
Large Hadron Collider 115
Larkin, Philip 75
law, legal 16–17, 19, 20–22, 33, 35–36, 47, 70, 78, 90, 94, 106, 123–125, 131, 143, 145
laws
　Asimov's 17
　Moore's 4
　Pasquale's 25
　Russell's 24
　Zeroth 17
Layard, Richard 91–92, 108
　Layard's 7 Factors Affecting Happiness 92
legal *see* law
legal personality 16, 20–22, 70, 123, 131, 143
Leibniz, Gottfried 3–4
Leviathan (Hobbes) 3
Liar's Paradox 130
Libertarian Utopia *see* the 12 Dooms
lie, lying 78, 95n14, 123, 130
Lipson, Hod xiii, 1–2, 45–46, 69, 111
Long Short-term Memory Recurrent Neural Networks *see* LSTMs
looms 3, 142
Lovelace, Ada 3
LSTMs 6, 143
Luther, Martin 88

MacDougall, Duncan 65
Machiavelli, Niccolo 132
machine, machines 2–5, 8, 10, 15–16,
        24, 31, 43, 45, 59, 70, 73–74,
        109, 111, 113, 119–120, 123, 130,
        141–142, 143
    machine ethics 119, 143
    machine learning 5, 143
MacIntyre, Alasdair 99
Manifesto, Cyborg (Haraway) 113–114
Manifesto, Robot (Poole) 124–125
Māori 21
Massachusetts Institute of Technology
        see MIT
materialism, materialists 33, 39, 43, 56,
        64–65, 67, 84, 141, 143
Matrix, the (movie) 91
matter, material 47, 53, 66–68, 100, 140,
        142, 143
matter, mattering 32, 90, 92, 99–100, 103,
        105, 108
Maxipok (Bostrom) 112–113, 143
Max-Pooling Convolutional Neural
        Networks 6, 143
MBTI 55
McEwan, Ian 81
McGilchrist, Iain 40–42, 56, 65, 68, 84, 87,
        105, 138, 140
Mead, Margaret 69
meaning i, 41–42, 44, 51, 66, 68, 74, 81,
        89–93, 100, 106, 108–109, 124,
        133, 142
memory, memories 6, 76–77, 84, 139,
        143, 145
mens rea 36, 143
Metamorphoses 2
metaphor 40–42, 87, 113
    dead 40, 140
metaphysics 39, 43, 64, 143, 146
microchip see chip
Microsoft 7–8
Midgley, Mary 16
Midrash 52
military, use of AI 17, 19–20, 83, 123, 125
Millbank, Paul 84
mimetic desire (Girard) 107, 144
mind 29, 36, 39–44, 46, 59, 64–69, 79, 82,
        139, 141, 142, 143

mind/brain theory 42, 68, 79, 144
mindfulness 68
miniaturisation 4
Mission Command (Bungay) 120, 144
mistakes i, 8, 16, 19, 43, 46, 53, 74, 77–79,
        81, 90, 94, 100–104, 106,
        108–109, 114, 118–121, 124, 139,
        142; see also err, error
MIT 4
mitigation, plea in 35, 145
monism, monists 65, 144
Monster, Overcoming the see 7 Basic Plots
mood, moods 53, 75, 87, 94n5, 100, 142,
        144, 145
Moore's Law 4, 144
moral 15–16, 21, 34–35, 46–47, 58, 70,
        77–78, 84, 104, 106, 109, 112,
        118, 121, 123, 131–132, 139, 147
morally 16, 22, 33, 35, 106
morality 34, 101, 147, 148
Moravec, Hans 30, 46, 144
    Moravec's Paradox 30, 46, 144
Morse, SJ 36
Moser-Wellman, Annette 85–86
MRI scans 43, 51–52, 56–57, 83
multiprocessor 6
Musk, Elon 17
Myers Briggs Type Indicator see MBTI
Mythology 81

Nagel, Thomas 43–44
nanobots 115
nanogenes 70
narrative 64, 80, 88, 100, 131, 132
naturalism 144
necessary, epistemology 53
Negative Capability (Keats) 87, 144
Nemesis 131, 144, 147
Neocognitron 6
-ness, as a definition of consciousness
        43, 47, 59, 131, 139
neural network 1, 5–9, 46, 116, 122, 140,
        143, 144, 145
neurobiology, neurobiological
        35–36, 58, 77
neurodiversity 103
neuron, neurons, artificial 1, 5, 9, 45–46,
        140, 143, 144

neuroscience, neuroscientist 35, 67
neuroticism *see* the Big Five
Nietzsche, Friedrich 132
Nones 93
normative, cf positive 53, 59, 107, 132
notation, effect on memory 84
nothing matters 73
novels, literature *see* story, storytelling

Obama, Barack 9
objectivity 55
observer *see* 5 Faces of Genius
Observer, Impartial (Smith) 78
obsolescence problem 29, 32
Odyssey 84
Ontogeny non-discrimination (Bostrom)
    16, 144
ontology, ontological 33, 39, 51–52, 59, 64,
    68, 139, 142, 145
ontological proof 64, 142
OpenAI 52
openness *see* the Big Five
Operation Bumblebee 86
optative mood 87
orbitofrontal cortex 56
organism 40, 43
ought/is (Hume's Guillotine) 53, 60n7
Ovid 2, 115
oxytocin 114

pandemic 87, 101, 105; *see also* Covid-19
paradigm shift 84, 145
paradox 30, 46, 130, 144
Paranoid Android, Marvin the 117
parenting 108, 113–114, 118
Pasquale, Frank 24
patterns 5, 6, 55, 86, 93, 105, 142
Penrose, Roger 47
perceiving *see* MBTI
personality
    legal 16, 20–22, 70, 124, 131, 143
    psychological 54–57, 75, 92, 116,
        118, 138
persons, personhood xi, 20, 21–22,
    33–34, 46, 52, 67, 69, 83, 123,
    125, 132
phenomenology, phenomenological
    43, 53, 55

philanthropy 112
philosophers, philosophy xiii, 16, 19, 34,
    36, 40, 42–45, 47, 54, 56–57,
    64–65, 67, 69, 70, 78, 81, 89,
    91–93, 106, 108, 130, 132, 139,
    140, 143, 144, 146
Philosophical Investigations
    (Wittgenstein) 83, 130
photographs 10; *see also* image recognition
phronesis 57–59, 145
Physicalism 65, 145
physiology 115
Picard, Rosalind 116
pineal gland, as the seat of the soul 67
Pinker, Steven 91
Pinocchio 2
Pixar 75
Plato 65–67, 74, 81, 109, 132, 141
playing 7, 30, 89, 90, 133; *see also* games,
    gaming
plea in mitigation 35, 145
Plots, 7 Basic (Booker) 80–82, 131, 146
Porn 30
Positive, cf Normative 53, 59, 107
posteriori, a 53
potentiality 66
predestination 90, 145
predetermination 145
preferences, personality 54–57
prefrontal cortex 56
pride *see* Ekman's Basic Emotions
principles
    AI 17–18, 24, 26n11
    Beijing 17, 26n12
    Bostrom 16, 69
    Pasquale 25
    Regulatory 17–20
    versus Rules 119
    Russell 24
Prisoner's Dilemma 118
privacy 18–19
probability 5, 9, 112–113, 133, 138, 143
problem
    alignment i, 9, 19, 113, 124, 137
    binding 41–42
    combination 42
    control i, 19, 23–24, 32, 140
    hard 40, 47, 142

mind/body 42, 68, 79, 144
obsolescence 29, 32
protein folding 7
processors 6
program, programming i, xi, 3–8, 22,
    24–25, 32–33, 44, 52–53, 56,
    70, 73–74, 77, 79, 86, 90, 93, 99,
    116–124, 130–131, 133, 141, 142,
    146; *see also* algorithms
programmer, programmers 8, 53, 56,
    74, 124
Propædeutic Enchiridion (Stephenson) 115
Property Dualism, cf Substance Dualism
    65, 140
Protector God *see* the 12 Dooms
proteins, protein folding 7, 137; *see also*
    AlphaFold
psychiatric 145, 146
psychological type 54–56, 116
psychology, psychologists 19–20, 35,
    54–55, 58, 67, 75, 78, 81, 91–92,
    105, 116, 121–122, 132
psychometric tests 54–56
psychopathy 145–146
    psychopathy scale (Hare) 145
punch cards 3–4
purpose i, 42–44, 66, 68–69, 89, 91–92,
    100, 106, 109, 124, 133
Pygmalion 2, 115

quale 44, 58, 83, 109
qualia 43–47, 54, 58–59, 66, 68–69, 101,
    130, 145
quantum entanglement 47, 120, 145
quantum physics 44, 47, 68
Queen, White 87
quest *see* 7 Basic Plots

rabbit/duck illusion 83, 130
radio 40, 83
Rags to Riches *see* 7 Basic Plots
rationality as computation 3, 57
Rawls, John 34, 147
realis moods 87, 145
reality 41, 51–52, 64–65, 90, 124, 131, 141,
    142, 143, 145
Rebirth *see* 7 Basic Plots
reCAPTCHA 10

recurrent neural network 6, 143, 145
regulation xi, 17–20, 23–25, 32, 109, 123,
    125, 132
    regulatory themes, principles 18–22
Reinforcement Learning 1, 7–8, 46, 77,
    116, 119, 131, 145
Relief *see* Ekman's Basic Emotions
religion, religions 42, 64, 68–69, 78, 87–88,
    92–93, 108–109, 121, 132, 143
remorse 78, 103, 145
repentance 78, 103
responsibility 16, 18–19, 21–22,
    35–36, 113
reversion *see* the 12 Dooms
reward 8, 56, 100; *see also* reinforcement
    learning
Riddell, Patricia 100
rights
    animal 16, 21
    human xi, 21, 67, 106
    robot 15–16, 21, 27n38, 123, 131, 135
Riley (*Inside Out*) 75
risk 9, 17, 19, 24, 31, 33, 36, 56, 59, 81, 88,
    92–93, 100, 112–113, 115, 118,
    123–125, 132
river 21, 44
robot
    Adam 73
    cognitive 5, 124, 139
    deterministic 5, 124, 140
    ethics 15, 119
    history 2
    I Robot (Asimov) 17, 26n8
    Manifesto 124–125
    rights 15–16, 21, 27n38, 123, 131, 135
    robot-ness 47, 59, 131
    social 2, 76, 116
    Sophia 2, 21, 32
robotics 2, 16–17, 21, 24, 46, 69, 111,
    138, 146
rogue chatbot 8; *see also* Tay
Rowling, JK 85
rules 3, 5, 7, 17–20, 21, 23, 31, 33, 52–53,
    58–59, 68–70, 78, 80, 89–90, 107,
    114, 119, 125, 130, 138; *see also*
    Principles
RUR, Rossum's Universal Robots
    (Čapek) 145

Russell, Stuart 20, 24, 47, 109
Ryle, Gilbert 43, 139, 141

Sadness *see* Ekman's Basic Emotions
safety 18–19, 22, 77, 93, 112–113; *see also*
    security
Sage *see* 5 Faces of Genius
Sandel, Michael 34
sapience, sapient 15–16, 70, 146
Satisfaction *see* Ekman's Basic Emotions
savoir, cf connaître 70, 139,
    146, 148
scenario *see* the 12 Dooms
scepticism 54
Scheherazade 104
Schmidhuber, Jürgen 8
Schrödinger, Erwin 47
Schulz, Kathryn 77
SciFi, SF 2, 17, 30–32, 74, 81, 89–90, 114,
    123, 132, 138, 145, 146; *see also*
    speculative fiction
scratch, program 4
search engine 10
Searle, John R 44, 51, 139
Second Sight 105
security 18, 22, 147; *see also* safety
Seer *see* 5 Faces of Genius
self-awareness 1–2, 15, 45, 69, 116–117,
    131, 146
self-destruction *see* the 12 Dooms
semantics, cf syntax 44
semiconductor 4, 147
sensing *see* MBTI
sensory pleasure *see* Ekman's
    Basic Emotions
sentencing 35, 145
sentience, sentient 10, 15–16, 21, 70, 118,
    121, 146
seven basic plots 80–81, 146
SF, SciFi 2, 17, 30–32, 74, 81, 89–90, 114,
    123, 132, 138, 145, 146; *see also*
    speculative fiction
Shakespeare 82, 86, 89
Shame *see* Ekman's Basic Emotions
silicon 4, 16, 147
sin 78, 118, 132
singularity, the 29, 146
Sistine Chapel 45, 84

Sixth Sense 20, 55, 74, 82–86, 90, 100,
    104–105, 108, 121–122, 142;
    see also Intuition
smartphone 4, 86, 107
Smith, Joshua K xiii
Sociopathy, sociopaths 146
software 3, 4, 74
Sokoban 9, 122
sola fides (Luther) 88
Song, Robert xiii, 33
Sophia the robot 2, 21, 32
sophistry and illusion (Hume) 39–41, 146
sorrow 91; *see also* sadness
Soskice, JM 40
soul, souls i, xi, 2, 42–43, 59, 63–71,
    71n1, 72n10, 74, 78–79, 84–85,
    91, 93, 109, 112, 115, 124, 129,
    131–133, 135, 137, 140, 142, 143,
    146, 147
source code i, 70, 93, 108, 131, 141, 146
spatial 69, 148
speciesist 33
speculative fiction 30, 146; *see also*
    SciFi, SF
spirit 63, 68, 88, 139, 146
spirituality 68, 109, 132
Spock 74
spooky action at a distance (Einstein)
    47, 145
Spufford, Francis 77
SRI *see* Stanford Research Institute
Stanford Research Institute 6
statements 17–22
    UNESCO 19–22
Steampunk 2
STEM 19, 105–106
Stephenson, Neal 30, 115
sterilisation 33
stochastic algorithms 5, 146
Stoicism 90, 146
Stoppard, Tom 40
story, storytelling 8, 17, 31, 70, 75,
    79–82, 89, 91–94, 97n64, 99, 104,
    106, 108, 116, 121, 123, 131, 141,
    142, 147
Stratego 12n23; *see also* DeepNash
subconscious 49n25, 82, 104, 122
subjunctive 87

substance dualism, cf property dualism
65, 140
Substrate Non-Discrimination (Bostrom)
16, 147
suffer, suffering 15, 42, 79, 118
superintelligence 31
supernatural 67, 143–144
surveillance 31, 34
switches 4, 8–9, 24, 90, 117, 147
syntax, cf semantics 44, 74, 142
synthetic reasoning 53

Taliaferro, C 64
Tay, chatbot 8
Taylor, SE 114
techne 57–59, 141, 145, 147
technology 4–6, 18–19, 21, 24, 29, 31, 34,
105, 116
Technomoral virtues (Vallor) 119, 147
Tegmark, Max 31, 45, 90, 112
teleology, teleological 43, 70, 91
Tenner, Edward 23
terrorism, and education 105–106
Test, Turing 10, 147, 139, 147
The Matrix (movie) 91
Theodicy 79, 147
theology, theologians 19, 33, 42, 52, 67–68,
78–79, 84, 93, 132
theory
Archetypes (Jung) 81, 137
Big Five Theory of Personality 54, 56,
118, 138
Fight or Flight 114–115
Hylomorphism (Aristotle) 66, 142
Language Games (Wittgenstein)
40, 68, 121, 143
Mimetic Desire (Girard) 107, 144
Theory of Intelligence (Cattell) 58, 121,
140, 141
Theory of Justice (Rawls) 34, 147
Theory of Mind 64–68 (*see also* mind/
brain theory)
Theory of Moral Sentiments (Smith) 78
thinking styles 54–57; *see also* MBTI
thought, as a process 3
Tinwell, Angela 20
toddler 1, 30, 69, 77–78, 144; *see also*
Moravec's Paradox

Tolkien, JRR 82–83, 132, 141
Tractatus Logico Philosophicus
(Wittgenstein) 130
tragic, tragedy 77, 80, 124, 131–132,
142, 144, 146; *see also* 7 Basic
Plots
transistors 4, 144
translation, by AI 44–45
transmitting 40, 83, 94
transparency in AI 8, 18–19, 22, 23
trichotomism 71n8
Turing, Alan 10, 129–130
Turing Test 10, 147, 139, 147
types
archetypes 80–81, 121, 137, 139
intelligence 57–59
mood 87
personality 54–57, 75, 92, 116,
118, 138
thinking 54–57

Uncanny Valley 20, 147
uncertainty 42, 74, 86–88, 90, 94, 105–106,
108, 122, 142
unconscious 30, 47, 81, 94, 105, 122,
137, 139
UNESCO 21–22, 124, 139, 140, 147
utilitarianism, utilitarian 32, 59, 90, 147
utility 99, 116

vale of soul-making (Keats) 79
Vallor, Shannon 120, 147
values 18–19, 68, 80, 91–93, 99, 108–109,
119–120
World Values Survey 91–93
veil of ignorance (Rawls) 34, 147
verisimilitude *see* uncanny valley
virtue
intellectual virtues (Aristotle) 57–58,
141, 145, 147
technomoral virtues (Vallor) 120, 147
virtue ethics 90, 107, 119, 148
volition 89–90, 93, 106–107, 120, 123
Voyage and Return *see* 7 Basic Plots

walking robot 45
weapons 19–20, 83, 123, 125
Weng, J 6

Whanganui River 21
White Queen 87
Wikipedia 52
Wissen, cf kennen 142, 146, 148
witchcraft 104–105, 122
witch-pardoning 105
Wittgenstein, Ludwig 40, 51, 68, 83, 90,
    121, 129–130, 143

Worldview 64, 101, 107–108, 112, 124, 131
wrongitioners (Schulz) 77

Yudkowsky, Eliezer 15

zero shot learning 69, 148
Zeroth Law (Asimov) 17
Zookeeper *see* the 12 Dooms